God and Primordial People

God and Primordial People

The Rise and Fall of Man and
Our Rescue through Christ

Paul Poulton

RESOURCE *Publications* · Eugene, Oregon

GOD AND PRIMORDIAL PEOPLE
The Rise and Fall of Man and Our Rescue through Christ

Copyright © 2018 Paul Poulton. All rights reserved. Except for brief quotations in critical publications or reviews, no part of this book may be reproduced in any manner without prior written permission from the publisher. Write: Permissions, Wipf and Stock Publishers, 199 W. 8th Ave., Suite 3, Eugene, OR 97401.

Resource Publications
An Imprint of Wipf and Stock Publishers
199 W. 8th Ave., Suite 3
Eugene, OR 97401

www.wipfandstock.com

PAPERBACK ISBN: 978-1-5326-4023-0
HARDCOVER ISBN: 978-1-5326-4024-7
EBOOK ISBN: 978-1-5326-4025-4

Manufactured in the U.S.A.

Unless otherwise stated, scripture quotations are from the Holy Bible, New International Version®, NIV® Copyright © 1973, 1978, 1984, 2011 by Biblica, Inc.®

Dedicated to The Lowe Family: David, Jeannie, and Jan
"God is not unjust; he will not forget your work and the love you have shown him as you have helped his people and continue to help them."
Hebrews 6:10

Contents

1. Divine Sculpting | 1
2. Migrants | 6
3. Simplicity Itself | 10
4. Sex-Driving Lessons | 13
5. God Said to Them | 20
6. The Great Awakening | 27
7. Dawn of Humanity | 31
8. Art for Art's Sake | 36
9. Dead and Buried | 39
10. Run Baby Run | 43
11. The Fall of Man | 46
12. The Competition | 53
13. Creation Groans | 59
14. The Center of Civilization | 68
15. Train Up a Child | 80
16. The Long-Livers | 87
17. Producing Fruit | 90
18. Educating Adam | 95
19. Made in the Image of God | 98
20. Forefathers | 104
21. Appointed to Die | 114

Contents

22. Faith | 117
23. Bad from Birth | 121
24. Bone and Flesh | 132
25. The Work of Our Hands | 137
26. A Clean Heart | 141

Appendix A | 145
Bibliography | 147

Chapter 1
Divine Sculpting

Michelangelo said, "Every block of stone has a statue inside it and it is the task of the sculptor to discover it." A human sculptor who slowly and skillfully chips away at a block of stone is similar to the sculpting of life by God who deftly worked away at the clay of the earth until it reached a state where he considered it "good." God, the sculptor, found the image of a human being in earth's clay and turned that human frame into a being made in his image.

The modern world is in a position to view the divine sculptor's work as no other generation has. Throughout previous generations many people believed that God created life, but preceding generations were not privy to the method and manner in which he worked—his *modus operandi*. We are now in that position, thanks to the fine work of archaeologists, geologists, paleontologists, and scientists, some of whom have faith in God: the Big Bang theory itself was first proposed by a Christian priest who was also a scientist.

Georges Lemaître proposed that the universe had a beginning—an observation he made from reading the Bible and working as an astronomer and professor of physics. Lemaître described his thoughts on the universe as "the Cosmic Egg exploding at the moment of the creation." Some people were not too happy with this theory. British astronomer Fred Hoyle, taking part in a BBC radio broadcast made a disparaging remark about the exploding universe, calling it the "Big Bang theory." The name stuck. Albert Einstein was also slow to accept Lemaître's expanding universe but when Edwin Hubble published his findings on objects observed in deep space, Einstein was quick to accept Lemaître's view.

God and Primordial People

Lemaître said, "Once you realize that the Bible does not purport to be a textbook of science, the old controversy between religion and science vanishes ... The doctrine of the Trinity is much more abstruse than anything in relativity or quantum mechanics; but, being necessary for salvation, the doctrine is stated in the Bible. If the theory of relativity had also been necessary for salvation, it would have been revealed to Saint Paul or to Moses."[1]

Lemaître makes a valid point. The Bible is concerned with humankind's salvation and not science, but the perceptive reader of the scriptures will garner enough information to acknowledge that the Bible and science can comfortably coexist. The precise wording of the book of Genesis and the meticulous work of scientists, each in their own way, offer insights into the creation of man. Scripture and science are far from being opponents and serve the common purpose of informing us of issues pertaining to their individual fields. We also see that the "fields" of scripture and science periodically overlap.

Genesis 1:24–28 announces the arrival of human beings. God called humankind "Adam," reminding them that they originally came from the "land," the same as all the other creatures. Adam is mentioned for the first time in the Bible in Genesis 1:26. English Bibles translate the word as "man," "mankind," or "human beings" but the Hebrew word is *Adam*. Adam, in the context of Genesis chapter 1, is a collective group. *Adamah* is Hebrew for "ground," so there is some wordplay involved—man named the animals but God named man (2:19; 1:26–27). The word human is in the same category as the word Adam and therefore reminds us of the ground. We see that the word human extrapolates its earthy meaning into other words too. "Humus" is dark, organic material that forms in soil. "Humility" means down-to-earth. "Exhume" means to dig something out of the earth. God has given us a permanent reminder of our humble beginnings in our name as Adam or Human.

In the early Proto-Indo-European language the word *ghomon* means "earthling" or "earthly being." This is helpful because if we look at the word ghomon we can see "human" in there, as well as "homo." Latin uses *Homo* from where we get "hominis" or "man." We see it in "homicide," meaning to kill a human. In French "man" is *homme* and in Spanish it's *hombre*.

We are from the genus Homo. The word "kind" is the biblical term for "genus." "Let the land produce living creatures according to their kinds:

---

1. Vecchierello, *Einstein and Relativity*, 24.

the livestock, the creatures that move along the ground, and the wild animals, each according to its kind" (Gen 1:24). We are Homo sapiens. Homo reminding us of the "ground" or "earth," and *sapien*, meaning "sapient" or "wise." Genesis concurs, informing us that there came a point when the creatures from the ground became Homo sapient—from the ground yet with the image of God upon us (27).

In his acclaimed book *Sapiens: A Brief History of Humankind*, Yuval Noah Harari writes, "What then drove forward the evolution of the massive human brain during those 2 million years? Frankly, we don't know."[2] When we humans struggle to comprehend, even with our massive brain, Genesis is happy to enlighten us.

Genesis 1:24 informs us that living creatures came from the ground: "And God said, 'Let the land produce living creatures.'" God doesn't say, "Let the land produce" a second time when man is made in his image, because he said that right at the beginning of the process—man comes at the tail-end of the procedure, which is what scientists tell us and Genesis confirms. God then says, "Let us make man in our image," not referring to the land producing at all (26).

We read, "And God said, Let the earth bring forth the living creature after his kind, cattle, and creeping thing, and beast of the earth after his kind: and it was so" (24 KJV). Notice the order: cattle, creeping thing, and beast. The root of the Hebrew word "beast" is *chay*, which means "living," and is sometimes used to describe God himself as the "living" God. Included in "beast" were early pre-humans. There came a point when God saw that the condition of some of the beasts had developed to a level where he could endow his image on them. Note that God doesn't say, "Let the land produce" again when man is made in his image, God now says, "Let us make man in our image."

We can't help but notice that beast is missing when God gives his reasons for making man in his image. "And God said, Let us make man in our image, after our likeness: and let them have dominion over the fish of the sea, and over the fowl of the air, and over the cattle, and over all the earth, and over every creeping thing that creepeth upon the earth" (26 KJV). The fish and fowl are there (God made them on his fifth day of creation). Cattle are there, and so are the creeping things, but no mention of beast. Science informs us that beast had developed (in its highest form) into man, and Genesis concurs. We do not expect the book of Genesis to highlight every

2. Harari, *Sapiens*, 9.

stage of evolution, God has given that job to scientists, but the omission of the word "beast," and the introduction of the word "man," informs us that the book of Genesis is still leading the way. Science will always trail behind scripture. When we begin to think that science has highlighted some new universal truth we have to stop in our tracks and admit that the Bible got there first. Science informs us that beasts developed into man and Genesis (with a smile on its face) makes provision for that transition.

If we think about God saying, "Let us make man in our image," the choice of words suggests that man is already there. If man were not already there God could have said, "Let us make man and let us make him in our image." But God didn't say that. The main point being made here is not the making of man, but the making of man in God's image. It is the "image of God" that is the focus of the sentence when God says, "Let us make man in our image." This statement seems to presuppose that the basic "man" is already there but that God is going to add one important final ingredient, which is spirit. A car manufacturer may make a stylish car, with an engine that runs nicely and an interior that is plush and ergonomic, but until a human being sits behind the wheel and drives the vehicle, the car does not reach the potential for which the manufacturer made it. The "human spirit" is the driver within each man and woman that enables us to reach the potential for which we were made.

Let's look at this scenario another way. Imagine a pool table on a ship with the natural lurching of the ship making the pool balls move and collide in an indiscriminate manner. The clashing of the balls would not seriously gain anyone's interest. But if we place a human pool player at the table hitting the balls skillfully with a pool cue we find that the interest of onlookers is awakened. The "spirit" that God placed within human beings is the skillful player at the pool table able to pocket the electrons within the human brain with consummate ease. The human spirit separates us from the animals whose instinct serves them well but it's nowhere near human beings' creative thought. To be human is far more than a biological machine. There is a driver in this hominid vehicle, there is a player at this anthropological pool table, there is a ghost in this biological machine.

Confusion arises in some people's minds when they read Genesis chapter 2 because biblical Hebrew doesn't have a pluperfect tense—a fact important for the Bible student to remember. Critics say that Genesis chapter 1 has the animals created before humans but chapter 2 has a human created before the animals; however, that objection disappears once we take into account the absence of pluperfect tense in Hebrew. Early Hebrew states the completion of an event but leaves the time of the event to be inferred by the context. "Context is king" is a saying that some Bible translators like to use; they say it because it's true. Hebrew tenses do not convey the time but simply the state of an action.

Genesis 2:7 (KJV) says, "And the Lord God formed man of the dust of the ground, and breathed into his nostrils the breath of life; and man became a living soul." This means, "The Lord God, who had previously formed man of the dust … " which is exactly the same as Genesis 2:19 that says, "And out of the ground the Lord God formed every beast of the field, and every fowl of the air; and brought them unto Adam to see what he would call them." The meaning being that the Lord God had previously formed the beasts that we read about in Genesis chapter 1.

Genesis chapter 2 naturally follows chapter 1 chronologically, and once we grasp that, then the events described in Genesis fall into place historically, scientifically, geographically, and theologically.

There is also another important aspect to the man Adam (in Genesis 2) being formed of the dust of the ground that will become apparent as we move forward.

Chapter 2
Migrants

THE MASSIVE HUMAN BRAIN may not be quite the trustworthy indicator of our ability to stand out in the league of life as we may think. We now know that the human brain is not, in fact, that massive. There are beasts that have bigger brains, and living creatures that have a better "brain-size to body-weight ratio," and animals that have a similar number of neurons, or far more: there are 86 billion neurons in a human brain and 257 billion in an African Elephant's brain. For some years the frontal lobes of the human brain were thought to be larger and therefore, perhaps, the feature that singled human beings out as being special among biological creatures, but that has now been called into question. An article called "Gorillas Agree: Human Frontal Cortex is Nothing Special," in *Scientific American* says, "The size of our frontal lobes, including specific frontal regions such as the prefrontal cortex, is nothing special."[1]

We learn from the scriptures that each human being has something further attaching itself to their being, something that a mere biological creature does not possess—a spiritual appendage to the organic apparatus known as our physical body. The human spirit was designed with the express intention of enabling its creator to relate to its owner—God could now talk to men and men could talk back.

Now, with the gates of communication open, we read in Genesis chapter 1 that God spoke to the people he had made, telling them to "Be fruitful and increase in number; fill the earth and subdue it. Rule over the fish in the sea and the birds in the sky and over every living creature that moves on the ground" (28).

---

1. Kaufman, "Gorillas Agree," para. 7.

Archaeologists, paleontologists, and geneticists have been informing us for decades that modern humans migrated throughout the earth from a local base. Genesis has been pointing us to the same scenario for far longer than decades: millennia ago man was told to "fill the earth."

The early chapters of Genesis sit well with science and archaeology. Genesis chapter 1 informs us that humans were hunter-gatherers (the Paleolithic Period), who followed the animals and ate from what naturally grew in the ground or from trees. They were under an edict from God to "fill the earth, and subdue it," which they did because we can see the evidence they left behind. Genesis chapter 2 informs us about humans settling down and learning how to cultivate crops (the Neolithic Period). The area where much of this agriculture took place is called the Fertile Crescent. The Lord God helped with some of the planting: in southern Mesopotamia he planted a garden.

Long before the garden was planted, humans lived a simple life. There were no agricultural mechanisms in place that helped sustain human life. God oversaw the sculpting of the planet we live on and the life that lived upon its surface and we note that he took exquisite care. The simplicity of each organism's ability to stay alive and pass on its genes to the next generation is a wonder at which we still marvel. How do insects survive the harsh winters? Their frames are a relatively tiny group of cells, yet somehow each summer there they are, and often out in force. It's amazing! Simplicity has coupled itself to complexity, and those tiny bunches of cells we call insects have continued to survive for millennia, dwelling tidily in the ecology of planet earth while they live out their brief lives.

Animals seem to fit snugly here on earth, able to sleep in their own skin. My dog is always ready to rush out the door at the mention of the "W" word. I am always careful not to mention the word "walk" until I've got myself completely ready. Because if I mention the word too early she will run around, jump up, howl, bark, and generally exhibit an unbridled enthusiasm to head out the door. The difference between my dog and me is remarkable. I need my proper walking shoes, the correct clothing for the time of year, the lead for the dog's collar, a hat or perhaps an umbrella. My dog needs nothing.

Dogs are equipped for whatever life may throw at them, so too are most animals. But we humans concoct all sorts of conventions that need to be adhered to before almost any undertaking we care to pursue can take place. As we read the first few chapters of Genesis the impression dawns upon us that humankind has moved some distance away from how we were originally asked to live. God wanted early man to live a simple life. He probably wants those of us who live in the twenty-first century to live a simple life too, but the "world" has grabbed us and we are too far into the depths of its machinery to find an easy way out.

Jesus sent his disciples out two by two and said to them, "Take nothing for the journey except a staff—no bread, no bag, no money in your belts. Wear sandals but not an extra shirt. Whenever you enter a house, stay there until you leave that town" (Mark 6:8–10). We seem to hear a faint reverberation of Genesis 1 in Jesus's words pointing us to a time when simplicity was life's backbone. The hunter-gatherer people were under an edict from God to "fill the earth," and each day as the people spread out God would provide the necessary sustenance for their biological health. Jesus recalls those days in his Sermon on the Mount, "Therefore I tell you, do not worry about your life, what you will eat or drink; or about your body, what you will wear. Is not life more than food, and the body more than clothes? Look at the birds of the air; they do not sow or reap or store away in barns, and yet your heavenly Father feeds them. Are you not much more valuable than they?" (Matt 6:25–26).

God fed early humankind as they migrated from Africa towards Europe, Asia, the Americas, Indonesia, etc. Some followed herds of animals that led them to where they needed to be. Others stayed where they were, in Africa, but Africa is a large continent and filling Africa would be their job. Provision was made for each small grouping of human beings to be fed and watered by the hand of the Almighty.

We also read that God told them to "have dominion over the fish of the sea, and over the fowl of the air, and over every living thing that moveth upon the earth" (Gen 1:28 KJV). God then said, "I give you every seed-bearing plant on the face of the whole earth and every tree that has fruit with seed in it. They will be yours for food" (29 NIV). Thereby explaining to the primordial people that they were to be, what we term, hunter-gatherers. The word for "dominion" in Hebrew means to "tread down" or "crumble off." There is no command not to eat meat, fowl, or fish in Genesis chapter 1. What do we suppose having dominion or ruling over the fish in the sea might mean? If we were to see a man at the beach standing in the shallows of the sea pointing to the minnows around his ankles and shouting, "I say unto you little fishes get thee hence from my ankles," we would grab our children and find somewhere else to paddle. God told men to crumble off some of the fish in the sea and not to worry about emptying the waters of creatures, there were plenty more fish in the sea.

God wanted to be active in the lives of the people he had created in his image. He desired to provide for them everyday. When we set ourselves up with vast provisions we rob God of the opportunity to supply our daily needs. The rich young ruler found it too hard to sell his possessions and follow Jesus—a temptation we may all face on different levels.

How do we know that God fed the people? We know because humans are still located across the face of the globe, all these years later—we got here somehow.

Genesis 1 helps us answer why humans first left Africa to migrate to the far reaches of the habitable planet. Why should they leave Africa in the first place? Conditions in Africa were favorable, contrasted with the icy blasts of Siberia and across the Bering Strait Land Bridge into Alaska. Why would people migrate such great distances?

Geneticists and palaeontologists seem to think that there were fewer than 10,000 people in Africa some 60,000 years ago. The first wave of migrants began to make their way to India, Southeast Asia, and Australia. A second wave appears to have set up base camps in the Middle East and southern Central Asia from where they moved on into Europe, Asia, and the Americas.

Sea levels were lower during the most recent Ice Age, which enabled people who were migrating from East Africa to walk across the land bridges to Indonesia and populate the Philippines and Australia, etc. (People may have also used boats to traverse the sea between landmasses that were relatively close to each other.) The reason the oceans were not as high as they are now is because the polar ice caps were larger in those days, meaning there was less water in the atmosphere and therefore in the sea, so people could walk across land bridges. People set out from East Africa around 60,000 years ago, and were in Australia by about 55,000 years ago. The earliest known evidence of human occupation in Australia is a rock shelter in the Northern Territory that is about 55,000 years old.

The time allowed for these migrations to take place could easily encompass 10,000 years, and for the arrival of human beings in the Americas, thousands more. Genesis highlights the reason people left their tropical homeland—their motivation came from the directive to "fill the earth, and subdue it."

Chapter 3
Simplicity Itself

Let us make man in our image. (Gen 1:26)

THE HEBREW WORD FOR "man" is Adam. The word can have a plural or singular meaning. When we read that God made "Adam" in Genesis 1:26 we know the word is used in its plural sense because verse 26 continues, "So God created mankind (Adam) in his own image, in the image of God he created them; male and female he created them." This verse informs us that we are not reading about the individuals called Adam and Eve that we read about in Genesis 2, for in chapter 2 only the man was called Adam, the woman was named Eve and called *ishshah*, meaning "wife" or "woman."

Genesis chapter 1 speaks of the human race in general, hence God told them on the day they were made in his image to "Be fruitful and increase in number; fill the earth and subdue it" (28), but concerning the individual Adam that we read about in Genesis chapter 2 we are told, "The LORD God took the man and put him in the Garden of Eden to work it and take care of it" (15). The individual Adam in chapter 2 was given a location and told to stay put and attend to his work, whereas the collective Adam in chapter 1 were told to migrate.

The people taking part in the exodus from Africa, 50,000 to 60,000 years ago, may have lived a simple life but they were not simpletons. God had endowed them with his image, they were biological entities, but not merely biological, there was something of spirit about them. These humans had the instincts that physical bodies need, akin to the animals that also have all their instincts embedded deep within their frame ensuring their

Simplicity Itself

species will survive. But these Adam (plural) had something more—a part of their being was immaterial.

Humans had originated from the "land" or "dust of the earth," identifying with other biological creatures, but human beings possess more than mere instinct, we have God's image stamped upon us. We are able to reason, laugh, and express ourselves with art, poetry, and song; we convey empathy, love, and worship. The oldest flute, made from the bone of a vulture, has been found in a Stone Age cave in Germany. The flute is dated at 40,000 years old.[1] Music, it seems, has been placed into the heart of men as a gift and a blessing. The genetic structure of a chimpanzee and a human are close, but on another level there is a massive gulf that cannot be bridged by physics or biology alone. Hence we are tested, on one hand we are far above animals and yet on another level we are the same. "I said to myself concerning the sons of men, 'God has surely tested them in order for them to see that they are but beasts'" (Eccl 3:18 NASB).

God's image upon Homo sapiens lifts us to a distinct and distant arena from all other species because a fundamental ingredient—spirit—is missing from other creatures. We operate on a totally different plane to the animals. Early modern humans were clever people who lived simply. And perhaps there is more wisdom in living a simple life than the wisdom we have in the modern world, with all our multiplicity of diversions from the moment we wake until our head hits the pillow at night, with maybe just one more look at a screen before we drop off to sleep. The early humans, who were following God's proclamation to spread throughout the earth, needed all their insight, wits, and intelligence to negotiate the terrain, the animals, and the danger that they would encounter. Their acumen, knowledge of nature, and ability to adapt are addressed by David Meltzer, an archaeologist at Southern Methodist University who notes that "These folks were extraordinarily adept at moving over the landscape."[2] The reason they possessed this remarkable ability to negotiate the landscape can, in some measure, be attributed to God who was working with them. "The Spirit of God moved upon the face of the waters" (Gen 1:2 KJV). The Holy Spirit moved during the primeval stages of the earth's development. He shaped and prepared the surface of the earth for when the creatures that possessed his image were to start their journeys upon it.

---

1. Owen, "Bone Flute," lines 1–4.
2. Pringle, "First Americans," para. 8.

God and Primordial People

God's Spirit would be a feature of daily life for the early peoples of planet earth. Each day's requirements would be provided, as needed, by his hand. When one of Christ's disciples asked him to teach them how they ought to pray, the disciple may have thought the answer would be long and complicated but Christ's answer was disarmingly simple. What has become known as the Lord's Prayer contains the line, "Give us each day our daily bread" (Luke 11:3). The request for daily provision was a way of life for planet earth's premier people. God had already spoken to them about food, it was a daily need that had been planned for by God as he shaped the earth in preparation for the people who would negotiate its terrain.

In *Scientific American*, Heather Pringle speaks of the first people to traverse the Bering Land Bridge making their way from Siberia into Alaska, saying, they "Dressed in warm, tailored hide garments stitched together with sinew and bone needles and armed with an expert knowledge of nature, the ancestors of the Paleo-Americans entered an Arctic world without parallel today."[3] These first Americans were called Clovis People, because Clovis, New Mexico, was where archaeologists discovered many of the early migrants' tools.

The paleo people's "expert knowledge of nature" would be a necessary skill for a relatively small group of human beings who were on the move. First Corinthians 3:9 (NASB) states that "we are God's fellow workers" and the primordial people of planet earth found that to be true. God was working with them, helping them survive the glacial movements of the most recent Ice Age, guiding their steps, and providing each day's meals. Simple trust in God would have been an everyday feature of their lives.

---

3. Ibid., para. 9.

Chapter 4

Sex-Driving Lessons

WE MAY FIND OURSELVES asking the question, "How, exactly, did God speak to these early human inhabitants of planet earth?" And this would be a good question to ask. There are several factors to the answer and we will look at three of them. The first component is easy to see if we look at the sea creatures and birds that were created on God's fifth day of working.

> God blessed them and said, "Be fruitful and increase in number and fill the water in the seas, and let the birds increase on the earth." (Gen 1:22)

God said this to the creatures he'd created by placing within them an inbuilt desire to reproduce—Genesis is giving us a little insight into the inner workings of God's creative process. But it is not only God who interacts with the animal kingdom. We often speak to animals: I tell my dog to "roll over" and she rolls over. The process of teaching my dog to roll over took a while and she would always expect a treat after obeying my request. I utilized the instinct within my dog to encourage a certain behavior from the dog.

God also taught animals to do some quite amazing things. We wonder, *how do birds know when and how to build their nests?* They have tiny brains, they don't go to school to learn, and yet they are able to make a soft, snug environment for their young. Birds make nests better than humans make nests, I know because I once tried to make a nest that I'm sure no bird would find acceptable. Birds take their time, methodically making fine reliable nests, while some humans struggle to make their bed. The Southern Masked male weaverbird builds a skillfully designed nest that is also used as a device for attracting a female weaverbird. The male bird selects a fresh

God and Primordial People

blade of grass, and then ties it to a branch. He then collects more grass and weaves the blades together using stitches similar to how we would sew pieces of material together. The bird uses both of his feet and his beak for this intricate procedure. The female weaverbird comes along to certify that his work is up to standard, and if his construction meets with her approval she will consent to reproduce with him and then use his bird-built nest to rear their young.

So we see that God's simple directive to reproduce comes with attendant extras; there is more involved than simply mating. God placed within the animal kingdom all the necessary skills needed for each species to flourish. We humans feel similar instincts within ourselves; there is a drive within Homo sapiens to reproduce. So when God spoke to people in Genesis chapter 1 he said something similar to what he had said to the animal kingdom, and we can still hear those words quite clearly because, from our adolescence on, the reproductive "animal instinct" placed deep within us alerts us to its presence, and sometimes quite forcefully.

But we need to consider something more. If we read Genesis 1 with care, we notice that God addressed human beings in a certain way and creatures of the animal kingdom in another. When he spoke to humans, Genesis tells us, "God said to them," which means he addressed them directly. We do not read, "God said to them" regarding the animals. When he spoke regarding the sea creatures and birds, we read that "God blessed them and said, 'Be fruitful and increase in number.'" God did not address them directly as he did human beings. God spoke in a different way to humans than he spoke to the other creatures, because humans, made in his image and likeness, could comprehend what God was saying.

There is a reason we have "being" after our species' name. Shakespeare wrote, "To be, or not to be: that is the question." "To be" means we have a self-awareness and knowledge that "we are." God said that he was "I am," we are made in his likeness and have substance at a deeper level than the beasts. The French philosopher René Descartes teaches that we can doubt almost everything, we can doubt that we even exist, perhaps we are in some kind of dream, after all when we are asleep we seem to think our dreams are real when in fact they are only figments of our imagination. Descartes points out that while we can doubt most things, there is one thing we cannot doubt, and that is that we are, in fact, doubting. We cannot doubt that we doubt. Therefore if we doubt, we have substance from which the doubt emerges. His famous saying, *"Cogito ergo sum"*—"I think therefore I am"—allows us to answer Shakespeare's question by saying, "'To be' is to be a human being." There is value and substance in our humanity.

So, a second way God speaks to us is through humans being made in his image. God's image within us is able to comprehend God's words and all their accompanying obligations. God's likeness and words are still reverberating within us because human beings notice that, in addition to our instincts, we also have a quality (God's image) informing us about our responsibility. If a human male desires to mate with a human female then offspring may result; provision will then need to be made for the mother and child. Human beings have a conscience that warns us about "appropriate behavior." We need the sex drive to be there but we also need a conscience to steer the "drive" in the correct direction, that we may know when it is appropriate to put that instinct into play. The man who goes around spreading his seed hither and thither will soon be ostracized by society, and mothers will soon be warning their daughters to keep well away from this man—he is a loser and a scoundrel, a worthless fellow who has fallen far below the standard set for human beings made in God's image.

I sometimes enjoy reading what naturalists have to say. (A naturalistic philosophy is a belief that only natural laws and forces operate in the universe; there are no supernatural or spiritual laws or forces at work.) Naturalists look at humanity and use their philosophy to explain why we behave the way we do. According to naturalists, we humans act like we do because there is an underlying instinct deep within the individuals that make up our society that we hadn't realized was so strong. There is some truth in what they say but it seems to me that the naturalist can easily minimize great swathes of human behavior, both good and bad, to the level of animalistic behavior. The naturalist and humanist may label "normal stimuli," such as "falling in love" as a mere chemical reaction designed to move the human species forward by means of procreation. The naturalist philosophy may also cause us to think that "supernormal stimuli," such as pornography is also from an underlying instinct. Perhaps it is nature's way of avoiding overpopulation. The naturalist philosophy seems to say that normal stimuli serves its purpose in pushing humanity forward and so does supernormal stimuli in its own way. But another person may simply label normal stimuli as "good" and super stimuli as "bad."

> Dress it up or call it "what the butler saw."
> It's always been with us but now more than ever before.

These are the first two lines of a song I wrote called "Porn." What we call pornography has been with us for a long time; from ancient Egyptian images that embarrassed the Victorian British explorers who saw them, to the biblical sisters named Oholah and Oholibah. We are told that Oholibah looked at images portrayed on a wall; she lusted for her paramours whose genitals were like a donkey's, and whose issue was like that of a horse (Ezek 23:20). Sometimes I wish the Bible wasn't so graphic and would spare us the details, but I guess that God doesn't shy away from telling us what we need to know. How church ministers got portrayed on TV as sheltered people protected from the roughness of reality I'm not sure, but it certainly wasn't through reading the Bible.

Let us be certain, God is extremely interested in human reproduction. God created the universe as a framework for life, and then he created life step by step. The pinnacle of all that hard work is Adam and as we have said, the Hebrew word for "Adam" can mean an individual or mankind; either way, like a wedding cake, a human male and a female stand on the top. God is keen, we might say exceedingly keen, to see humanity continue to endure throughout the ages he has planned for planet earth. His opening communiqué to us was, "Be fruitful and multiply."

We know God is concerned that humans multiply because of the strong sex drive he placed within us. Drive is a good name for it because it drives us on. For instance, a young man keeps his eyes open for a suitable girl, and we know that there are certain qualities that a young man finds attractive in a woman. It will help if she is slim, has good muscle tone, and is intelligent. The naturalist will label this behavior as the human species "choosing the best specimens" to ensure its survival. Being overweight is not good for our health and so the sex drive doesn't immediately make it appealing. Lad-mags, as a general rule, entice young men to their magazine by putting a slim girl rather than a stout girl on the cover. Similarly, when a girl wears a low-cut top a naturalist would point out that the girl's body language is saying, "Young men come hither and look at my ample bosom, see how my breasts will provide much milk for fine strong babies to feed on." In some ways the naturalist has a good point, God has placed within each of us instincts that we follow whether we realize it or not.

The sex drive is a good quality to have—a blessing, for "God blessed them and said to them, 'Be fruitful and increase.'" But with most vehicles that have a "drive," steering correctly is a necessity. If humanity somehow loses its grip on the steering wheel of the sex drive then it will careen out

Sex-Driving Lessons

of control for lack of competency in the driver's seat. And who wants to be a passenger in a fast moving vehicle with no one capable at the steering wheel?

God has entrusted us with our very own sex drive, and because we are made in God's image we find it incumbent upon us to steer it correctly. When I first passed my driving test and was let out on the roads with a car, I took extreme care every journey; I was in charge of a fast moving heap of metal that could cause some damage if not controlled. Nowadays, I may be more relaxed about driving because it's a natural part of my life, but I know that at any moment I could crash my car if I don't steer it according to the rules of the road. Being made in God's image gives us some inherent rules for steering our sex drive along the route it's meant to go. There are some wrong roads and dead ends that we can end up in if we don't take care.

There are a number of sex-drive rules of the road and here let me mention three of them.

1. The sex drive is there for reproduction, but the benefits that surround it are many—loving family, security, etc. Some people, I am told, don't have much of a sex drive. I'm prepared to believe that. Paul, in the New Testament, spoke about some people having the gift of being single (1 Cor 7:7). But it seems the rest of us have been given a task to perform—the matter of propagating the human race. The picture is a lot bigger than just looking at marriage from a reproductive point of view, of course. Some couples may marry and, for a number of reasons, don't have children. God gives some people the blessings of marriage without children, and he has his reasons. But we are not now looking at the big map, just a part of it where some people may lose their way. God's first words to us were, "Be fruitful and increase in number" so if an adversary desired to cause unrest between God and human beings, God's first words to us would be a good place for the adversary to start. Pornography can be a life-long port of call for some people, they never move on, never get married, and never reproduce. The naturalist may say that the low ebb people report feeling after looking at pornography is put there by nature to move them on in life, to actually find a mate and reproduce. The naturalist philosophy may again be correct but the Bible gives us a little more insight—the forces of nature were placed into the great scheme of things by God. We are not being spoken to by blind random chance; we hear instead the words of our heavenly creator. The Christian perspective of monogamous marriage is that

the delight of only ever seeing one woman naked outweighs the desire to see many (and vice versa from the female viewpoint).

2. The sex drive has a strong engine and doesn't need the help of husband-hunting females revealing their buxom bosoms in low-cut dresses. Most young men are keenly aware what is hidden beneath the exterior fabric of a nice dress and don't need any help from young ladies who would like to remind them. The same goes for a young man showing off his abdominal six-pack at the first excuse. Young girls aren't as oblivious as you suppose. There is a virtue known as modesty and it has an enticing quality all of its own.

3. God gave us the sex drive and also made us in his image so there are two factors involved. Therefore, we are able to conclude that our sex drive is not meant for making babies at every given opportunity. Babies need providing for, hence God made "the family": one man impregnating one woman with offspring ensuing. The man, while not the one screaming giving birth or being able to suckle the infant, can use his strength and wits to be hard at work erecting a shelter or building a home, gathering food, and providing clothing for them all. The glue holding the family together is a quality called "love," something that the naturalists may find hard to define in a purely analytical way. God is love, so we have inherited this trait as a part of his image in ourselves. Love is strong enough to keep us together, but somehow, as the course of human history reveals, our hearts began to harden.

At the beginning of this chapter I said we would discuss three ways that God spoke to the early human inhabitants of plant earth. We have covered two of the ways and will now focus on the third.

God said, "Let us make mankind in our image, in our likeness."
(Gen 1:26)

Both "image" and "likeness" have a visual connotation as their first meaning. Therefore we have to seriously consider that God walked with men in the early days of humanity similar to the way Jesus walked with men in Israel. "Whatever the Father does the Son also does" (John 5:15). As we read Genesis chapter 1 we see a picture of Elohim already on earth, ready and willing to lead and guide earth's primordial people.

We cannot discount that God spoke to human beings through his physical presence in an intimate face-to-face encounter. Genesis goes on to relate how God walked in the garden, spoke with Cain and Abel, walked with Enoch, and shut the door on Noah's ark. He ate lunch with Abraham and called him friend. Early humans in their innocence and simplicity would have known the presence, leading, and appearance of the Lord. "He tends his flock like a shepherd: He gathers the lambs in his arms and carries them close to his heart; he gently leads those that have young" (Isa 40:11). As time progressed God's presence among us was lost. And there was a reason that God removed himself.

Chapter 5
God Said to Them

WE CAN STATE FOUR ways that God may have spoken to people in the early days of humanity.

1. Through instincts that he placed within each human being.
2. Through intuition that humans received from being made in his image.
3. Through an anthropomorphic representation of himself.
4. Through his Spirit.

God spoke in detail to human beings but animals were directed only by the instincts within them. Towards the end of Genesis chapter 1 we read that God spoke to the people about nutrition. This is information that humans were able to hear and comprehend, while animals can neither listen to instruction (without engaging their instincts) nor comprehend sentences. God spoke to the early human beings about their daily provisions, and the human beings listened and took note.

> God said, "I give you every seed-bearing plant on the face of the whole earth and every tree that has fruit with seed in it. They will be yours for food. And to all the beasts of the earth and all the birds in the sky and all the creatures that move along the ground—everything that has the breath of life in it—I give every green plant for food." (Gen 1:29-30)

Notice that humans are addressed directly as "you" or "yours" but the beasts and birds are not. God speaks to human beings. We are made in his image and can relate to him and he to us. God and humans can have a relationship.

God Said to Them

In Genesis chapter 3 we are presented with a scenario of God walking. Adam and Eve hid because they heard the sound of the Lord God walking in the garden. There are other examples of God appearing to men in an anthropomorphized way—Yahweh appeared to Abraham, and lunch was prepared. Let's recount once more that when Genesis tells us that we are made in God's image, there may be a number of ways that this phrase applies to us, but the first meaning of "image" is something we see, an object to be looked at; an image is an optical expression. The word "likeness" is also used. "Let us make mankind in our image, in our likeness (1:26). In Hebrew the word for "likeness," *demuth*, means "*similitude* of external appearance," leaving us to draw the conclusion that God could have spoken to the early humans the same way he spoke to Adam and Eve or Abraham: in an anthropomorphized expression of himself.

God loved early humans, they were the first people on the planet, and he gently led them. Isaiah 49:10 supplies us with a little insight into God's heart: "They will neither hunger nor thirst, nor will the desert heat or the sun beat down on them. He who has compassion on them will guide them and lead them beside springs of water." As modern humans made their way out of Africa, God was with them, tending and brooding over them. He provided for them and interacted with them.

God blessed them; and God said to them. (Gen 1:28)

We need not think that God said this but once and that was it, he may have spoken to the people many times, and in a similar way Jesus may have told the same parable more than once to different audiences. The disciples were well acquainted with the sayings of Jesus and were easily able to recall them, perhaps because they had heard each of the parables several times.

When the early people of planet earth needed help, help would be forthcoming; God would not leave these folk made in his likeness without assistance. Angels could have also played a part in those early days. "For he will command his angels concerning you to guard you in all your ways" (Ps 91:11). Let's not think that angels only helped out in later days. The probability of "helping angels" appearing in former times is greater because the earth is fully inhabited in the twenty-first century. We have scaled its furthest reaches, so help is not needed as it was in those early days. And when help is needed these days there are more than enough humans to mount the necessary rescue mission.

God and Primordial People

We may not be giving ourselves to fabulous conjecture in assuming that the LORD was present with the early human beings in a similar way to how he was present with Abraham when he sat down under the shady trees of Mamre and ate lunch. There is no real reason why he could not have been, and we need to factor this possibility into our thoughts. God could have spoken to early man in a form they could easily recognize.

Abraham and Moses came thousands of years after primordial people but perhaps a little more light may be thrown on to the way God related to human beings in earlier times when we hear God say to Moses, "I am the LORD. I appeared to Abraham, to Isaac and to Jacob as God Almighty, but by my name the LORD I did not make myself fully known to them" (Exod 6:2–3).

Abraham knew the name of Yahweh, or at least the Akkadian version *Ea*, pronounced *eyah*, but God's appearance to him was limited. Names were important in ancient times because they revealed something of the character of the person. God had not revealed his self-existent nature that the word "Yahweh" depicts.

The great I Am.

He is!

Yahweh—he who needs no apparatus to support his being.

God explained this to Moses but not to Abraham. In fact, Abraham was quick to prepare lunch for Yahweh and his two companions as if Yahweh needed the food. As we move on from Genesis to Exodus God begins to teach Moses, and us, about the nature of the LORD. The essence of his being is not material—he is Spirit. We cannot see spirit but he who is invisible made everything that is visible. Moses initially saw God in a burning bush and not any sort of anthropomorphized representation. Humans were beginning to understand that what is unseen is more important than what can be seen. God's revelation of himself to humans was a gradual process.

Abraham saw God as Elohim or we could say as "an elohim." Elohim is usually translated in Bibles as "God" (singular) because the context of the surrounding words demands it. The word "elohim" can also mean that we are talking about a class of beings called elohim (plural). Elohim is used in a similar way to the word "human," which means a class of particular beings—human beings. I am a human (singular), and I belong to the class of beings called human (plural). Elohim is God (singular) who belongs to a class of beings we cannot see, such as angels, who are also called elohim (plural). Bibles sometimes translate elohim as "angels," meaning *"divine ones.*" Elohim can even be translated as "human judges," such as in Exodus 21:6, "his master must take him before the judges." Here the NIV translates elohim as judges, so too does the King James Bible. Abraham knew Yahweh well, but even so, he did not have the knowledge about God that Moses would later receive.

We should also note that the Lord "appeared" to Abraham, Isaac, and Jacob. We know he appeared to Abraham as a man, not a human man, but a man of some sort. Angels can also appear as men. The people who saw Yahweh and the angels at various points in human history seemed to recognize that they were not ordinary men, they were elohim—a different class of being than human beings. This seems to be the way the Lord God appeared to the patriarchs prior to the time of Moses. God mingled with men without his glory shining through, similar to Jesus walking among people, and the people took their time before realizing exactly who was among them.

In this way God was able to speak and help the family of early human beings whom God had recently endowed with his image. The simplest meaning of the word "image" implies that early humans looked like elohim, and therefore elohim looked like human beings. Although God wasn't a human being, he looked like one in order that he may reach out to them and start the relationship between human beings and himself. As time progressed humans learned that God is not of this world, he is Spirit. God did not want human beings to make any sort of image of himself. After all, human beings were made in his image so there was no need for carvings, paintings, engravings, models, or graven or cast images of who he was, such items would be known as idols.

Humans are made in God's image and that is the only image God wants us to have. Colossians 1:15 explains to us that "The Son is the image of the invisible God." Jesus is the image of God, so any manmade images of God will fall spectacularly short in representing who God is. Genesis chapter 1 makes provision for Christ to be born—"Let us make man in our image" (26 KJV)—Christ was a man and he was "the image of God."

Perhaps we are not privy to every word that God spoke to primordial people, but Genesis 1 does give us the general picture. We can use our own experience of life to provide the obvious context—something the writer of Genesis assumes we will do.

God and Primordial People

> Have dominion over the fish of the sea, and over the fowl of
> the air, and over every living thing that moveth upon the earth.
> (Gen 1:28 KJV)

God is talking to human beings in the verse above, and that tells us that "every living thing" to be dominated does not include humans. The humans are asked to do the ruling over—the dominating. The implication of this statement cancels out any provision for human slavery. Humans are asked to dominate the creatures, brute beasts, or what we know as the animal kingdom. Humans are not asked to dominate other humans. Human beings should have mutual respect for each other whatever gender, race, or circumstances in which they may find each other.

Once the people had begun to spread out over the landscape the early humans were probably filled with wonder and joy on seeing another human being—people were few in number and scattered across the planet. So meeting up with other human beings would be a reason to rejoice. Archaeological investigations suggest that primordial family groups of around 20 to 25 people would traverse the landscape and these groupings would assemble together at prearranged meeting places for a celebration at periodic points in time, maybe annually or every few years. When the time for the assembly was finished the family groups would disperse again. However, as the ages progressed, and for several reasons, people lost the delight of connecting with other people, and today we may be tempted into thinking that other people are an intrusion into our lives that may cause us vexation. If we could revisit the pleasure of seeing another human, the modern world would be a different place. The early humans experienced God's love, showing them tenderness and compassion, and the human beings themselves would exhibit that tenderness for each other. In one way each human being is a representation of God, because we have his image or stamp upon us. For this reason when we welcome a stranger we can view it as welcoming God. "With the tongue we praise our Lord and Father, and with it we curse human beings, who have been made in God's likeness" (Jas 3:9). "Truly I tell you, whatever you did for one of the least of these brothers and sisters of mine, you did for me" (Matt 25:40).

God also said, "I give you every seed-bearing plant on the face of the whole earth and every tree that has fruit with seed in it. They will be yours for food" (Gen 1:29). We need to note that there is no restriction on eating meat. We draw a distinction between animal life and plant life because it is plain to see. But humans who eat plant-based food actually eat small animals inadvertently, such as tiny creatures that have lived on the plants.

God goes on to say, "To all the beasts of the earth and all the birds in the sky and all the creatures that move along the ground—everything that has the breath of life in it—I give every green plant for food" (30).

We see a distinction between the food supplied for humankind and the food appointed for animals. Humans eat seed-bearing plants and fruit from trees, and generally, animals who are not hunters feed on grass and leaves. So the fundamental supply of food for animals is derived from plants, shrubs, and trees, and the animals' predators eat the plants as a by-product of eating their prey that processed the plants into protein. Genesis marks out the color "green" regarding the animals' feed, by which we understand that buffalo, cows, deer, giraffe, goats, sheep, etc., forage, graze, or browse grasses or shrubs. The birds are also singled out for a mention—anyone who has tried to sow a new lawn with grass seed will know how quickly birds appear to devour the seed. Birds also eat creatures such as earthworms; we have all seen birds tugging juicy worms out of the ground. The worms themselves eat rotting leaves, fungi, and bacteria. If a food source is decaying, or vaguely organic, worms are probably willing to eat it. The birds eat the worms that have processed the decaying matter into protein and valuable nutrients for the birds. When worms or birds expel their waste they provide some fine fertilizer; we see that all things "living" take their natural place in helping earth's ecosystem run smoothly.

Let us consider for a moment that God has made some creatures to be predators and some creatures to be prey. The prey usually outnumbers the predator group by some measure: the more prey, the more predators. The numbers of each group tend to find their own sustainable equilibrium. Paleolithic man had no domesticated animal herds of their own, so the balance of animals in those days would be as nature intended it to be. Both prey and predators have a part to play. Cattle, for instance, trim excess grass, while predators trim excess cattle. So the predators sustain themselves on grass via cattle.

Land-dwelling creatures live on a foundation of plant-based vegetation in one way or another, which is what Genesis chapter 1 tells us. Sheep, deer, and cattle eat vegetation, and humans eat some of the sheep, deer, and cattle; we eat the vegetation that the animals have processed into protein. God made predators so that the protein-yielding livestock would not overrun the earth. Their numbers needed to be stabilized. Human beings tend not to eat creatures that hunt, such as lions, dogs, or eagles, as they are what Noah called "unclean" animals. Carnivores eat other animals, so a carnivore's protein is secondhand, not acquired directly from vegetation but from prey.

There are studies these days that inform us a diet high in meat is not necessarily the best for a human being's health but we also know that a little animal-based protein, especially fish can be helpful to our biological frame. Perhaps we should note what Genesis 1 relays concerning our food. God spoke of the plants and fruit in relation to food and that should give us human beings insight that fruit and vegetables are an important part of our diet.

Noah was told to take seven pairs of each clean animal and one pair of each unclean animal onto the ark. So if we think of the herbivores as clean and the carnivores as unclean we see that Noah released a ratio of 7:1 back into the Mesopotamian wild. The ratio of prey to predators fluctuates: if the population of prey decreases the knock-on effect will produce a decreased predator population, and usually, not too long after the dip in prey numbers. When the prey population enjoy strong growth the predator numbers will also increase. A ratio of 7:1 seems like a good prospect for predator group growth. This ratio also leaves some room for humans to take part in some hunting too.

Chapter 6

The Great Awakening

In him was life; and the life was the light of men. (John 1:4 KJV)

WE FIND OURSELVES WONDERING, *when was God's image bestowed upon Homo sapiens?* Modern humans seem to have been around for 200,000 years but whether they had the image of God upon them 200,000 years ago needs some thought.

In the late 1900s a number of geneticists thought the human genome contained between 80,000 and 100,000 genes, the high number related to our biological complexity. Gradually, as more research was done, the number of supposed genes came down to 35,000. But in 2004 when the human genome was fully decoded and analyzed the number was found to be nearer to 20,000—a shock for some researchers. On October 21, 2004, *Science Daily* reported that "National Human Genome Research Institute (NHGRI) and the Department of Energy (DOE), has published its scientific description of the finished human genome sequence, reducing the estimated number of human protein-coding genes from 35,000 to only 20,000–25,000, a surprisingly low number for our species."[1]

God shaped the biology of humanity very carefully and added his divine "life and light" to that biology, teaching us that a human being has a dimension that biological entities do not have. We have many predecessors in the evolutionary chain, and quite a number of them share over 50 percent of our DNA sequences. The scriptures teach that the spark setting humanity apart from other species came not from nature but from supernature. Biology is the framework in which human spirit resides. When our

---

1. NIH, "Researchers Trim Count," lines 2–5.

biological frame dies we have another framework in which to reside. The Apostle Paul says, "we know that if the earthly tent we live in is destroyed, we have a building from God, an eternal house in heaven" (2 Cor 5:1).

The Neanderthal race died out, so too did Homo erectus and Homo antecessor and others from the Homo genus, but they were not what we call "modern humans" or "Homo sapiens," rather we may term them as human subspecies. Some of the subspecies were a part of the building blocks that God used on the way to making man in his image. Geneticists say that a very small percentage of Neanderthal DNA seems to be present in some humans. When God told the humans to replenish the earth (Gen 1:28 KJV), the word "replenish" could refer to replacing the early species or subspecies from the genus Homo. So modern humans, with their integrated spirit, replaced previous Homo models.

> It is the spirit in a person, the breath of the Almighty, that gives them understanding. (Job 32:8)

God bestowed his image on humankind and called them Adam. Then Genesis sums up the whole long process of life's development.

> So God created mankind in his own image, in the image of God he created them; male and female he created them. (Gen 1:27)

We remember that the Hebrew word for mankind is Adam, and in Genesis 1:27 *ha-adam*, meaning "the human," or as we would say these days, "the human race." The human species is made up of two distinct sexes: male and female. Genesis 1 teaches us that both sexes are contained in the word "Adam"—"male and female he created them." Genesis 5:2 also makes it plain, "Male and female created he them; and blessed them, and called their name Adam." Both male and female were called Adam, and they were both human. We would suppose this to be the case because science, archaeology, and paleontology confirm what Genesis chapter 1 teaches us. Genesis chapter 2 moves on to explain the "generations of heaven and earth" where one particular Adam is spoken of, because one particular Adam began the process of heaven meeting with earth, fulfilled when Christ came among us and told us that "No one has ever gone into heaven except the one who came from heaven—the Son of Man" (John 3:13). Notice that Jesus calls himself the "Son of Man," meaning "Son of Adam," thereby completing the process that started with Adam in Genesis 2.

Genesis 1 points out the story of human beings ("Adam" in the plural sense) migrating, which began late in the Middle Paleolithic Period and continued into the Upper Paleolithic Period. Humans were asked to fill the earth. The particular dispersal from Africa that we are looking at began around 60,000 years ago. So although that could be the point at which God added the ingredient that put such a gulf between us humans and the animal kingdom, in my opinion God's image fell upon humankind earlier. Genesis 1 gives us the précis of what God said to modern humans but there could have been a long time period before humans were ready and able to migrate; after all, first and foremost, there was some multiplying of the human species to be done and then came the charge to "fill the earth."

We should not understate the importance of God's image being bestowed upon humankind even if we cannot place the event in a specific time period. Instinct can take a species a long way and can accomplish some marvelous feats: we have seen parrots that seem to count, kangaroos that box, and monkeys that paint, but none of these feats come close to the reasoning ability of a human being. "Creative thought" signals that something immaterial has attached itself to the physical brain. Our brains have a mind that is intangible in the material world—something "other" than this material universe. Spirit cannot be measured within the laws of physics, and it cannot be experimented upon in a laboratory. Spirit, or what scripture refers to as our "heart," came to us from outside this universe, not from within it, hence our "heart" remains elusive. Some materialists are keen to deny its presence, but atoms trying to fathom out atoms has never sounded likely, whereas spirit figuring out the layout of the house it lives in has always been the better option for discovering truth.

We may not be able to precisely state the time that humans were endowed with spirit, but people who read the Bible will be aware that the "heart of man" is something that is spoken of as other than our biological body. Jesus said, "Don't you see that nothing that enters a person from the outside can defile them? For it doesn't go into their heart but into their stomach, and then out of the body" (Mark 7:18–19).

Jesus pointed out to us that the heart is not a part of the body. He was not talking about our physical heart but the "heart of man," the center of our being, the point at which decisions are made. And there we have the root of the matter: the spirit or heart of a man is the well from which freewill springs. God has freewill, and humans have it too, it comes as a constituent ingredient of being made in God's image. However, care must be taken because freewill can lead us into trouble as well as lead us into joy. Freewill can be lost: a man can gain the world but lose his soul. There are addictions waiting like a fisherman's baited hook, addictions that will take away our freedom, all they need is for someone to take a bite of the bait and then the addiction gets to work on eroding the freedom that that human being was given as a gift.

God is extremely interested that we are free, for there are many other "gods" out there that would love to hijack our journey through this world.

Chapter 7

Dawn of Humanity

GOD'S SPIRIT BREATHED UPON Homo sapiens and self-awareness dawned upon humanity, enabling humans to be aware of the spacetime in which they resided—a capability to slice through the framework they inhabited. A human was able to work within nature and also be able to coexist with super-nature. Animals are a part of the fabric of nature and therefore unable to disentangle themselves from it. Human beings, however, have both nature and super-nature and are able to view both aspects. Biology and spirituality belong to human beings but animals have only biology.

Life began its journey towards this event long ago, and with the dawn of human self-awareness God was able to relate to creatures with a depth that no form of biological life had been capable of before. Proverbs 8:1 tells us that "wisdom" called out to human beings. And also, "I raise my voice to all mankind!" (4). Humankind was raised from the dust of the earth as wisdom, prudence, and knowledge were given to them.

The creation of the universe, with all its diffuse multifaceted natural spectacles and creatures, was a project in which the Lord had taken the keenest interest. Genesis tells us that God "saw it was good" long before humanity appeared on the earth. God's enjoyment of the whole creative process would be immense. We know the universe took a long time to get to where it is now. Plasma is one of the four fundamental states of matter, the others being solid, liquid, and gas. The universe first began as plasma, it took 370,000 years for simple Hydrogen atoms to form within the plasma and then gravity got to work forming stars. The stars eventually yield other types of atoms. The stars are "atom factories" that God uses to make the atoms and molecules needed to form planets and life. We can see the process still occurring in the current stars.

Let's not think it is simply through us humans that God finds satisfaction. However, we can see that humanity was the end product of the physical universe and that God was working towards that goal as each creative day finished and the next phase began. Our physical biology reflects our spiritual position—human beings are stand-up-straight bipeds, unlike the hunched quadrupeds. Humans are also able to look at the heavens immediately above their heads, unlike the animals that look along the horizontal plane of the earth or downwards to the ground—Jesus "looked toward heaven and prayed" (John 17:1).

The finishing touch to human beings was not a biological adaptation. The genetic sculpting process of humans had taken many thousands of years, that's how biological improvements occur, but this new addition was spirit, so its placement within the human race would not need to follow the biological route. Spirit came from a location outside of spacetime and once spirit was placed into Homo sapiens they could then truly be called human beings. As one of their celebrated writers would later say, "To be, or not to be: that is the question." Once spirit was added to the human frame the "being" could truly know itself and know others and simply "be." A human being's body enabled him to negotiate the valleys and hills of the earth, while his spirit enabled him to traverse other plains not seen with physical eyes. The Apostle Paul summed it up like this, "So we fix our eyes not on what is seen, but on what is unseen, since what is seen is temporary, but what is unseen is eternal" (2 Cor 4:18).

The completed human being had included in his person a quality that was not physical at all. He was not merely a collection of chemicals, or an assemblage of atoms; he was greater than a biochemical organism. Yes, he had a body, with instincts similar to other animals, but the human spirit was an addition that animals did not have. This spirit was not subject to the natural laws of physics, and spirit is the part of man that God was ultimately interested in, because God himself is Spirit. God and man could now relate on a new level, they could know each other, experience each other, love each other, and connect to each other. Furthermore, what each person was able to achieve with God they could also achieve with each other because each man and woman is made in God's image. "Whoever claims to love God yet hates a brother or sister is a liar. For whoever does not love their brother and sister, whom they have seen, cannot love God, whom they have not seen" (1 John 4:20). Jesus prayed for those who follow him "so that they may be one as we are one" (John 17:11).

Homo sapiens' lofty ascent into a creature that bears God's image was not without its dangers. A human being's spirit is what enables him to choose, it is from where his freewill springs. Spirit is what makes a man sum up his options and then choose one. Great care should be taken with a spirit.

A human being's spirit cannot be dissected like a body. We have heard that the soul is somehow intrinsically stitched into the spirit. Hebrews 4:12 explains that the word of God is so sharp that it can penetrate precisely enough to separate the soul and spirit. Perhaps we ought to think of it like this:

- A body is natural.
- A soul is the life force attached to the body.
- The spirit is annexed to the soul.

So the soul seems to be the go-between with the body on one side and the spirit on the other—a sandwich of body and spirit with soul in the middle.

The body dies; a fact we are all aware of: biological entities die. Death is a part of this natural world. The Bible teaches us that soul and spirit can also die. Physical life and death is a factor in the natural world, and God uses it to teach us about spiritual life and spiritual death—a lesson that has always been the Lord's priority. God warns one particular man (Adam in the garden) that his soul and spirit can die. "But from the tree of the knowledge of good and evil you shall not eat, for in the day that you eat from it you will surely die" (Gen 2:17 NASB). The Bible seems replete with warnings. "The soul who sins will die" (Ezek 18:4 NASB).

A stark warning reveals itself in the Bible. A particular individual seems to lose his humanity and regress to a former period of evolutionary growth. By the decree of God, the King of Babylon, Nebuchadnezzar, exchanged his human understanding for the instincts of an animal, and he lived with wild animals and ate grass like an ox. For seven years his body was drenched with the dew of heaven and his hair grew like the feathers of an eagle and his nails like the claws of a bird. Finally, he did what human beings are able to do and looked up to heaven. "At the end of the days I Nebuchadnezzar lifted up mine eyes unto heaven, and mine understanding returned unto me" (Dan 4:34). This world leader wrote all these events down that you and I may read his words and consider, "I, Nebuchadnezzar, praise and exalt and glorify the King of heaven, because everything he does is right and all his ways are just. And those who walk in pride he is able to humble" (37).

Jesus taught that "Flesh gives birth to flesh, but the Spirit gives birth to spirit" (John 3:6). So we can presume that self-consciousness descended on individual human beings suddenly rather than the slow way that biological life-forms evolve. Perhaps akin, though not the same, as when the Holy Spirit descended upon the apostles on the day of Pentecost.

A generation of people suddenly receiving the ability to reason would involve some practical and emotional implications. For instance, what happened to the parents of the generation that suddenly was able to think for themselves? We can safely presume that the number of humans who had this awakening was not great. Hominds had been looking after their young for many generations, just as apes and other animals nurture their offspring. If the generation that received "spirit" was young, the realization they were different to their parents would not take long to reveal itself. They would be clever young people who knew what their parents did not know. And perhaps there's not a lot new there, because young people these days often believe they know better than their parents—except in this case it was true. The young people who possessed this knowledge grouped together and made a life for themselves, with God's gracious and loving hand guiding them. Their parents' generation passed away and the small group of humans made in God's image began to fulfill their commission from God. We know that hominids from the Lower Paleolithic Period (early Stone Age) did not live as long as those in the Upper Paleolithic Period (late Stone Age).[1] The "wits" humans had been given would now enable them to use their wisdom to catch prey and figure out where and when the best food sources would be appearing. They no longer had to rely purely on instinct to survive. The Upper Paleolithic Period gave rise to a "flourishing of early human culture."[2]

These early humans began to relate to each other in a way that no other creature had before them. At first they had no formulated language to speak, but they did have a basis for communication, which they had inherited through the evolutionary process. Animals can communicate by using a variety of sounds or movements. Sea lions maneuver their bodies in various positions to communicate. A honeybee uses its waggle dance to inform the rest of the hive where a food source can be found. A deer may alert

---

1. Koerth-Baker, "Who Lives Longest?," para. 5.
2. Ibid.

its herd of a possible predator by snorts and stamping its hooves. Primates can use sounds, smells, and visual indicators as forms of communication. Many other animals are able to prepare each other through some form of communication. So the first human beings to be self-conscious had their inherited armory of sounds and body language, but they would soon realize they needed a lot more communicative ammunition at their disposal.

The exodus from Africa began around 60,000 BC, which is within the timeframe that linguistics think language began to develop. As each group made their way out and into the larger world, habitats would help to shape the words that the humans began to formulate. A hunting party may need to communicate over hundreds of meters so different pitches work better in certain environments. Some sounds carry well over a particular terrain; all this would help shape the languages that each group would develop as a part of its social interaction. Some languages have more consonants than others and a number of vocabularies have more vowels. The terrain each group belonged to or found themselves traveling in played its part in helping to shape the languages that we now hear throughout the world.

There is reason to believe that God also helped these early tribes of people extend their communication skills. Genesis chapter 1 tells us that God spoke to the people, although he did not have a lot to say to them. But that is in keeping with the fact that their reservoir of words, sounds, and body language were still at an early stage.

The basic communication skills would not take too long to build upon and each group of Homo sapiens would come up with words for each different circumstance.

Chapter 8
Art for Art's Sake

WE NORMALLY CALL THE period before the invention of writing "prehistoric." I suppose there is little use in us asking why the early people of planet earth didn't write about what happened to them. For one thing, they had very few words to write down, and secondly, the written word was a long way down the list of "putting first things first." Writing would eventually arrive at the top of humankind's "to-do" list. This happened when men found the need to record transactions and communicate over great distances with each other (about 5,500 years ago). Although writing had not yet arrived as an important skill to attain, doesn't mean that no records were kept.

Men, made in the image of God, found the need to express themselves. After all, God is creative and we have inherited that trait. In those early times, some men found they were gifted in certain areas of expression, which is no different to today. I myself am fairly poor when it comes to drawing anything, but I am a capable musician. In early times those gifted in music would have found some satisfaction in listening to their own rhythmic footsteps, as they walked along the soft thud of each step would have a poetic resonance that not everyone would notice, only those whose area of creative expression revolved around sound. In the evening when men and women had laid their children to rest, they would experiment with rhythms, perhaps hitting the ground with sticks, or drumming on fallen tree trunks. All sorts of interesting rhythms would ensue. Perhaps some of the folk would experiment with their own vocal cries, marrying a tune with rhythm. Others found delight in the vibration of air that was blown into a hollow bone and found they were able to change the pitch of the note by inserting holes along the bone. Music contained a strange satisfaction for human beings.

Some people found they could scratch a two-dimensional likeness of life onto a surface. The high degree of accuracy used in the drawings enabled those who looked at the etchings to relate them back into a three-dimensional view of reality.

Human beings have a predisposition for art. We cannot hear the music that was made in those early days but we are able to view the visual art of primordial people. We may not be able to read any written accounts left by early humanity but our premier mothers and fathers have bequeathed their artwork to us.

The earliest artifacts revealing workmanship of an artistic nature have been debated, but there's a consensus of opinion that such workmanship existed 50,000 years ago. This is known as the Upper Paleolithic Period. In Africa bone artifacts, including the first art, appear in the archaeological record. Further afield, utilitarian objects have been found with patterns on them, there was little practical need for this time-consuming artwork, and so we can safely presume that early humans were interested in art for art's sake.

The beautiful abstract art of Cueva de las Manos, Santa Cruz, Argentina, where hand after hand has been used as a stencil on the cave wall seems to suggest that the people from those days are waving to us. In the Tanzanian rock art we see slim human figures in interesting scenarios, which are quite lovely to gaze upon. Ancient rock art is found around the world and most of it can be recognized as human art that displays quality, tasteful art that wouldn't look out of place in a modern gallery.

The comic picture we sometimes see of savage cavemen hitting their future brides over the head with a club and dragging them off by their hair is not held up by archaeology. What we find in the caves of the cavemen are not remnants of brutality featuring the cracked skulls of females but expressive evocative etchings upon their walls. The two views of the savage caveman and woman on the one hand and the peaceful family who spend their leisure time painting seem diametrically opposed to each other.

The aesthetic quality of the stenciled hands of humans on cave walls reaches out to us down through the millennia. Perhaps Prehistoric Man is not prehistoric at all, they have left us a message, they communicate with us still. "We are as you are," they cry, "here, see our hands reaching out to you—our beloved sons and daughters." Their saluting hands echoing through the centuries, "Fare ye well, our children, live strong, be gentle, and grow in the life you have been given."

Refined techniques of dating have placed some of the cave wall art to around 40,000 years ago, (roughly the same timeframe as musical instruments that have been found). In the cave of Pech Merle near Cahors in France, two spotted horses can be seen, painted about 25,000 years ago. The horses have an ethereal aspect assisted by the irregular placement of four human hands. These people may not have been able to write words but they still wrote. A person who looks seriously at these paintings will be touched by the yearning and sentiment extending towards them.

Art transports us. Art lifts us to another plane. Art is human. Art is spirit reaching out to spirit through the interface of the material world.

The people, it seems, were learning from their great teacher who had accompanied them and gently led them.

> He tends his flock like a shepherd: He gathers the lambs in his arms and carries them close to his heart; he gently leads those that have young. (Isa 40:11)

The people too, were expressing themselves with a gentleness that was worthy of being made in God's image. Fine art needs to be created with care and gentleness. Much later in human history when the earth was well populated and the written word was commonplace we read that the fruit of the Spirit is gentleness. (Not forgetting love, joy, peace, patience, kindness, goodness, faithfulness, and self-control.) Gentleness is an important quality for a human being to possess.

> Let your foot fall lightly on the ground
> Quelling the urge to throw your weight around
> Walk humbly; enjoy the art of living
> Not grasping or grudging, but cheerfully giving
> Tread meekly and let your words be few
> Draw close to God and he will draw close to you
> Being rough has little merit, it's not what we're made for
> Bulls in china shops have no finesse, they simply wreck and gore
> A soft touch and a careful hand sets a man apart
> A human who's discovered that gentleness is an art[1]

---

1. Poulton, "Let Your Foot Fall," 2017.

Chapter 9
Dead and Buried

NONBELIEVERS AND BELIEVERS ALIKE have debated how primordial people became religious. Evidence that ancient people were aware of something other than this material universe seems irksome to some modern minds. The general ethos of modern skepticism seems to be "We know better now," and yet billions of people around the globe still consider themselves believers in some sort of religion, even in these "enlightened" times.

Spirit resonated with human beings as soon as it was administered to them. Spirit is something other. Spirit is a supernatural immaterial quality that allows humans to see themselves as something set apart from nature.

The Bible tells us that during the early days of humanity God looked after the Adam (plural) he had made in his image. He gently led them and provided for them. Their vocabulary would be tiny at first but perhaps they didn't need reams of words to comprehend divine love. God managed to impress them with his loving nature.

We would imagine that Homo sapiens needed to live in a basic practical manner simply to stay alive; theirs would be a utilitarian lifestyle. Yet, from the earliest human times people across the world seemed to share a numinous ("arousing spiritual or religious emotions") quality that each person could relate to. Beads, tools, items from daily life, figurines or other markers were sometimes buried with the dead, known as "grave goods," these artifacts suggest that the person dead and buried would appreciate these goods in some way after their death.

Organisms die—which has been apparent from the dawn of life itself. If organisms reproduce, then those same organisms must die and make way for their offspring. Otherwise there would be an unacceptable and ridiculous proliferation of species, and lack of space would quickly become an unyielding obstacle. A stable and balanced population growth is held in place by the death of biological organisms from lowly microbes all the way up to humans. But the intangible aspect of a human being is not integral to the physical universe because human spirit did not evolve through organic means. Modern humans from around 50,000 years ago seemed to understand that a feature of being human transcends our physical existence; they placed grave goods with their dead to mark this fact.

The grave goods would have been a sacrificial offering because some of the items buried would have a practical use to those still living, but so strong was the passion of the people to give something to the deceased that they were willing to make the sacrifice. People feel strongly about death, and if God's teaching was being grasped by the people of those early times then it could be that the grave goods were not so much an item for the dead to use while they were dead but an item for them to use after they had been resurrected.

The resurrection has been a long-held belief among human beings. "And after my skin has been destroyed, yet in my flesh I will see God" (Job 19:26). We act out death and resurrection every night when we go to sleep and every morning when we wake up. Early on, humans began to grasp that there was a divine message in each day's drama.

The doctrine of the fall and original sin (with its annexed views on what death means) was formulated by Augustine at a time in the early fifth century when the Pelagian controversy had erupted. Pelagianism is the belief held by a monk named Pelagius that original sin did not taint human nature. Augustine thought that human nature was tainted and proceeded to make his point by saying that even infants who have not been baptized will be condemned, though they will not suffer all of hell's pains. Augustine used a rather heavy theological hand to combat Pelagianism. Pelagius may have swung too far in one direction, while Augustine may have swung too far in the other in his attempt to combat the unrealistic propositions of Pelagius. Thus we are left with issues that the church is still dealing with. Differing positions of original sin have percolated down to us and we can end up with sections of our thoughts about the fall, human sinfulness, and death that are not always easy to fathom out.

Before the "doctrine of the fall and original sin" became a part of church dogma, Christians only had the Bible and the early church fathers who occasionally taught and shared their views on the subject.

Dead and Buried

> As for humans, God tests them so that they may see that they are like the animals. Surely the fate of human beings is like that of the animals; the same fate awaits them both: As one dies, so dies the other. (Eccl 3:18–19)

So, according to the Bible, death is a test. This theme is highlighted in the early church writings. Irenaeus (AD 130) in his *Against All Heresies* (book III) seems to suggest that death is God's way of mercifully helping us in our journey into the life of God.

We often look on death as something to be feared and avoided at all costs; perhaps we should not. Death may be a blessing given to human beings on their journey towards "eternal" life. After all, as we have seen, we act out the scenario every night and day. At night we lay our bodies down in the unconscious stupor of sleep, and while we are in this state we are no use to man or beast, but then as the morning light breaks with its shining rays, so do we, we rise and shine. Suddenly the immobile inactive and inert body that has been supine through the watches of the night is upright and energetic and ready to get on with the day's adventures. The whole scenario seems to be a picture of death and resurrection—a sign that we need to take note of, particularly perceiving that we do not fear sleep; in fact we often long for it. Jesus himself called death sleep; so did the Apostle Paul. Sleep is a simile. God doesn't always use words when communicating to people. As he led the early men, women, and children of the Paleolithic Period without many words, he leads us too.

This view of death is something we read in the scriptures but it seems we are slow to understand its meaning. When Jesus reached Jairus's house the mourners were already in place, Jesus stepped in and said, "Stop wailing, she is not dead but asleep" (Luke 8:52).

Being alive and being dead have another meaning when viewed through God's word. "God, who is rich in mercy, made us alive with Christ even when we were dead in transgressions" (Eph 2:4–5). Early man seemed quick to pick up on this point, and placed symbols in the graves of their loved ones, knowing that biological death is one more station on the journey, and not the journey's end.

Scripture's teaching—that life and death is a spiritual state: we can either be dead in our sins or alive in Christ—has ramifications for the church's divergent doctrine of the fall. The whole universe helps us grasp spiritual truth. A time will come when day will break and as Solomon said, the "shadows will flee away" (Song 4:6). While we are on earth we see the shadows and not the realities themselves, so even biological life and death take their place as a part of the shadows.

Biological death has always been a part of natural life; we would not know what spiritual death was if we did not know what physical death was. "The wages of sin is death" (Rom 6:23). Adam (in the garden) was told that the day he ate from the tree of the knowledge of good and evil would be the day he would die. But he didn't die on that day, so God must have been talking about some other kind of death. Jesus said, "Whoever lives and believes in me shall never die." But we still die a physical death, so Jesus must have been talking about some other kind of life. This is the message of the Bible—humans, who are made in God's image, can partake of the life of God if they choose to do so.

Chapter 10
Run Baby Run

THE LIFESTYLE OF THE first human beings that God breathed into was higher than our modern-day lifestyles. These days we tend to think that we have progressed far beyond our ancestors but perhaps in certain ways we have not. Rather than climbing higher we may have fallen far lower. Yes, we have many forms of communication and information and amusement: digital screen games, TV soap operas, movies, and social media. We have an abundance of fast food and many labor saving devices: escalators and elevators; cars, trains, and planes. But from another angle we have lost much. Many of the games we play and the TV episodes we watch are addictive, and social media can be a source of grief rather than connecting a happy coterie of friends. With the labor saving devices we have, such as door-to-door motorized travel, suitcases with wheels, escalators and elevators, in addition to present-day life promoting hours of sitting, we do nothing to encourage muscle growth but rather lend a helping hand to muscle atrophy. The lifestyle lived by simple, gentle folk who were first endowed with God's image may surpass our way of life by several leagues.

Our first human parents were fit and healthy, their diet was varied and nutritious. They would walk and run in pursuit of food. We have seen some quadrupedal animals move very fast, their two-leg advantage means they can sprint faster than us. However, the story is different when it comes to longer distances because humans can outrun most land animals. The human cooling system relies on many sweat glands and minimal body hair; animals tend to overheat over long distances. Furthermore, our two legs mean we can change the gears in our breathing pattern while we are running; animals run on all fours and their breathing pattern is regulated by their gait. Technically, quadrupeds synchronize their respiratory cycle for locomotion at a constant rate of one stride to one breath in both the trot and gallop. But humans differ from quadrupeds. We bipeds can employ several patterns of breath-to-stride cycles when we run—three strides to one breath, two strides to one breath, one stride to one breath, three strides to two breaths, and so on. The ability we humans have to change our breathing patterns, coupled with our superb cooling system, means that we are the favorite when it comes to distance running. All we have to do is give chase and an animal will eventually tire and give up in exhaustion, making the creature easy to capture. This procedure may take several hours, or longer, but when early humans followed God's advice to dominate the creatures that moved upon the earth (Gen 1:28) they found they could have dominion and were actually the superior long-distance runners.

Human feet are designed to run: our big toe lines up neatly with our other toes; apes' feet are more like a hand, with a gap between the big toe and other toes. Our big toe enables us to effectively lift off on each stride as we run—the big toe is the last thing to leave the ground. We have certain ligaments and tendons that behave like springs that are essential for running; these ligaments for running are not found in apes. Our narrow waist enables us to swing our arms, helping us to run straight and efficiently. If a food source is available to runners, covering the distance of a marathon and further is within our reach. Even if there's no fuel intake our muscles can store about twenty miles' worth of glycogen.

Our first human forefathers and mothers made use of these abilities; they were designed to run. The gluteus maximus, the largest muscle in the human body, is engaged primarily when we run, whereas it is hardly used when we walk. When I'm out on a long run in the woods I sometimes imagine I am a part of an ancient hunting party. They would enjoy the atmosphere of being together in pursuit of a protein source that, once captured, would be good for their families for several days. Thinking like this always helps me run.

Hunter-gatherers were people on the move. They explored their location and knew they were surrounded by beauty—ponds shimmering in the woodland, grasslands weaving and waving in the wind, the distant spires of granite mountains dotted with dark green shrubs, acacia trees with their umbrella-like canopy that would provide welcoming shade. They saw sapphire skies topped and tailed by streaks of red, gold, and turquoise adorning the sky at sunrise and sunset, evoking pictures of the eternal home where Elohim lived. They would occasionally meet other groups of Homo sapiens with whom they had no competition because they, all alike, were made in God's image. Rather, they would be willing to share what they had and offer hospitality. Then the small groups would move on. The journeying lifestyle that God gave to early man was a lesson in itself—here on earth we are on a journey, this is not our eternal home, we are heading somewhere. God was speaking to early humans through their daily lives. We modern-day humans may also find that the circumstances of our lives have something important to teach us if we can take a step back and see the larger picture.

God spoke to the people in Genesis chapter 1 and the people listened to what God said. The life God had given human beings to live was an adventurous, yet peaceful, way of life. The climate of the earth they walked on was different from the conditions we experience today. The Pleistocene Epoch ended about 11,500 years ago, marking the end of the glacial phase of the most recent Ice Age. In those early days of humanity the earth's climate was affected by extended polar ice caps. A larger percentage of the world's water was ice, so rainfall was low. Europe received approximately half the rainfall it gets today, and the rain fell mostly in the summer months, which were 4 to 8 degrees cooler than today. The tropical areas of the world were not as they are today. Water held in lakes was common in dry regions, particularly in the subtropics. Sea level was lower in those days, and the sea temperature was colder, making cyclones not so prevalent as they are today. The climate was less arid and the desert areas smaller with vegetation that would help to stabilize the dunes.

We call our present geological epoch the Holocene, which started 11,500 years ago when the glaciers began to retreat.

Chapter 11
The Fall of Man

God created mankind upright, but they have gone in search of many schemes. (Eccl 7:29)

GENESIS CHAPTER 1 REVEALS no "Thou shall not" commands being issued to early human beings. We do read that humans are asked to reproduce and to eat—two things that human beings seem more than willing to do. They were also asked to fill the earth—traveling and exploring also comes fairly naturally to us humans. When we get some free time during a holiday period we often travel somewhere. There were no instructions to early humans about not stealing, cheating, hurting, or killing.

Debate continues among archaeologists and anthropologists concerning the evidence of whether prehistoric people were either violent or peaceful. From a scientific perspective no easy conclusion, it seems, can be made. If we look at the subject from a biblical point of view early man was morally upright, although their noble and virtuous behavior hit a serious setback at some point.

From the "dawning of consciousness" people, being of an upright nature, had no use for commandments. They did not steal because they did not want to cause grief for a fellow human. They did not cheat because they wanted their fellows to prosper. When someone in their community prospered everyone rejoiced. They did not commit adultery because when they fell in love they remained true, there was no thought of being unfaithful because "eros" love was satisfied only with their particular beloved. The image of God was upon them without any contamination from evil influences. Human beings are ultimately,

The Fall of Man

> Created to be like God in true righteousness and holiness. (Eph 4:24)

Commandments were superfluous, because God's will was done on earth as it was in heaven among humans in their primal communities. Righteousness prevailed among the initial human beings. We ought not to suppose that they never had anything go wrong—a person may have accidentally trodden on someone's toe. All sorts of practical mishaps could have taken place, but upright men would bear no grudge nor treat anyone differently because they had been affected in an adverse way by someone's behavior. The "commandments" were always intended to be written on our hearts and not on stone tablets. Proverbs 3:3 says, "Let love and faithfulness never leave you; bind them around your neck, write them on the tablet of your heart." We have fallen a long way from those early days and reading the instructional writing within us is not always easy, but in each human being that writing is still there, written on our hearts since the primordial days of humankind. If we search deep, we will see it. Some people may have huge quantities of rubble covering that writing and the accumulated dross will need to be removed, but once the debris has gone they should be able to read that writing again.

Although God gave early men and women a wholesome and peaceful life, the scriptures reliably inform us that a malevolent influence was hiding in the shadows waiting for an appropriate opportunity to spill its bile into human life. The "serpent" is made known to us in Genesis chapter 3, and is introduced with a history of malign craft attached to his person. He has been calculating, cagey, and canny for some time. God's image being conferred upon humans may have been the reason for the serpent's rebellious waywardness.

The human era that Genesis chapter 1 speaks of is not necessarily easy for us to date, but if we pick the story up from when the human beings began to migrate, about 60,000 or 50,000 years ago, we can say that the serpent would be looking for opportunities to encourage humans to follow his own schemes from that time. There is reason for us to suppose that humanity's fall from grace began imperceptibly at first, but after a time the peacefulness humans enjoyed started to fray around the edges.

We have already mentioned "the fall of man" and much has been spoken about the doctrine over the centuries; the early eastern Greek churches had a different view to the western Roman church. As we noted, Augustine of Hippo helped shape the western church's view and several muddles have ensued. Augustine taught that un-baptized infants who die are sent to hell because of original sin. The Eastern Church had a different view of original sin and called their version "ancestral sin," meaning their ancestors sinned but that didn't necessarily mean we are culpable for their sin. The Eastern Church did not suppose that guilt was passed down through the generations but rather that each individual bears the guilt of their own failings. So a baby dying before baptism did not become a problem area and they rarely spoke about it.

There are other areas in the doctrine of the fall that turn into a bit of a metaphysical quandary for those who want to walk that route. Those who do attempt to tread that path may find themselves stuck in a philosophical debate that hinders Bible study rather than enhances it. I've heard people debating "once saved always saved" and "freewill and predestination," which seem to boil down to the age-old philosophical debate of determinism and human freedom.

We know that biblically, humanity was created in an uncorrupted upright manner, but Satan and his angels offered an alternative choice to the human race. The option Satan proposed was not based on love, kindness, and faithfulness. And human beings, eventually, decided to look into the option Satan had on offer. The simple life was forfeited and the "schemes" Solomon spoke about took precedence. Somewhere along the line "life and death" took on a new facet for the human beings who listened to the serpent. Death had originally been given to human beings as a help and encouragement for them to use their freewill in a righteous manner saying, "In view of the fact we will die, how then ought we to live?" The serpent changed this human rallying cry into the dissolute, "Let us eat, drink, and be merry for tomorrow we die."

The Apostle Paul wrote,

> All have sinned and fall short of the glory of God. (Rom 3:23)

Notice that Paul used the word "fall" in that scripture. Most Christians are aware that "the fall" affects us all in some way, although there is a range of thought about exactly how our fallen nature affects us. Take Gregory, the fourth-century Archbishop of Constantinople, who is well known as a Trinitarian Theologian and still influences modern Christians; Gregory taught that infants are born without sin. However, most theologians recognize that Gregory hasn't got that correct and that humanity has a flaw and furthermore we have it from our earliest years. Jesus himself made it quite

The Fall of Man

plain. "He did not need anyone to testify concerning man, for He Himself knew what was in man" (John 2:25). So Jesus knew that something lurked "within man." The picture this verse paints is that the something "in man" is not at all good. Jesus was not afraid to point out our true nature.

> If you, then, though you are evil, know how to give good gifts to your children, how much more will your Father in heaven give good gifts to those who ask him! (Matt 7:1)

Augustine helped to develop the doctrine of fallen humanity. It seems that since Irenaeus (in the second century) started talking about the subject of sin resulting from the fall of man, the doctrine has had a spectrum of adherents, from a few who think our fallen nature is a slight deficiency, to others who say we are totally depraved. The truth seems to lie somewhere in the middle. We are marred, we have a fault, but it is also apparent to fair-minded people that some of our fellow men and women are capable of acting in a good and upright manner and sometimes even in a heroic manner.

God told Jeremiah to go to the potter's house and watch him work (Jer 18). When Jeremiah watched the potter he noticed that the potter marred the first pot that he was working on so he made another pot from the same clay. The lesson was aimed at Israel who had let their blemish lead them astray, but we ourselves are also marred by our own sins and transgressions, so the lesson of the potter making a new vessel from the spoiled one is a good picture of fallen humans. We must be born again because the life we have from our first birth has been marred, so we need, as Jesus put it, new wineskins because the old ones will crack.

Humans have a tendency to veer off course; we are free agents who can become our own despotic gods. Moses pointed out, "They are not His children, because of their defect" (Deut 32:5). The King James Version translates "defect" as "spot," which is the Hebrew word, too. Humans are marred with a spot or blemish. The reason we have a tendency to veer off course is because the "spot," or the "law of sin and death," is at work in our lives. Originally, "God created mankind upright, but they have gone in search of many schemes" (Eccl 7:29). A piece of fruit that has a blemish will start to erode and rot from that point—sin works its way through us starting from our blemish.

Paul takes us back to the dawn of humanity and mentions that from our creation we have been able to view God's goodness saying, his "invisible qualities—his eternal power and divine nature—have been clearly seen, being understood from what has been made, so that people are without excuse" (Rom 1:20). Paul then proceeds to inform us what befell early humankind.

> Although they knew God, they neither glorified him as God nor gave thanks to him, but their thinking became futile and their foolish hearts were darkened. (Rom 1:21)

Paul uses the word "became," which is important. We can see that there was a time prior to "people having futile thoughts and dark hearts," and the "prior state" was the condition in which men and women were created—upright in character, which Solomon pointed out to us in Ecclesiastes 7:29. How long this prior state of uprightness lasted we cannot be precise about. But the Apostle Paul has some insight in this matter: he was caught up to heaven and saw visions and revelations from the Lord. And from his lofty position Paul had a good view of events previous and also events future. He speaks with authority about humankind's early days.

> Although they claimed to be wise, they became fools and exchanged the glory of the immortal God for images made to look like a mortal human being and birds and animals and reptiles. (Rom 1:22–23)

Figurines start to appear in the archaeological record around 35,000 years ago. Archaeologists tend to think that the figurines represent some sort of deity and label them "ritual objects." In the case of the figurine widely known as the Venus of Willendorf, found in France and dated to roughly 28,000 years ago, little is known about its cultural significance; however, it is one of 144 female figurines surviving from the Paleolithic Period.

Figurines from the Neolithic Period include the Mesopotamian Ubaid lizard men, noted for their unusual reptilian features. Both male and female figurines have been found depicting snake or lizard-headed humanoids with exaggerated shoulders and "coffee bean" reptilian eyes. These objects turn up in cemeteries near Eridu, Ur, and Uruk, the present-day country of southeast Iraq—ancient southeast Mesopotamia. Archaeologists named the figurines "Ophidian" because their faces resemble snakes. Archaeologists acknowledge that the use of the figurines is unclear.[1] They appear both in tombs as well as in settlements but the background and meaning of what the serpentine figures depict is puzzling to some archaeologists. Other people explain the ophidian figurines with conspiracy-type stories of aliens visiting earth or a race of lizard people who once inhabited the planet.

---

1. Streit, "Re-evaluating the Ubaid," 93–95.

The Fall of Man

What some people find bewildering is explained by the Apostle Paul who tells us that certain images made by men were "reptilian" in nature. Paul, in Romans chapter 1, highlights how humankind fell and particularly points us to reptiles in his description of manmade idols.

The Bible student will be quick to acknowledge that the timeframe and location for the reptilian figurines runs concurrently with the serpent in the garden of Eden. Both the serpent and the garden of Eden date to the early sixth millennium BC (Neolithic Period). But, for the moment, let us continue looking at Paul's discourse and the biblical perspective of what happened at the fall of early man.

So, "although they claimed to be wise, they became fools and exchanged the glory of the immortal God for images made to look like a mortal human being and birds and animals and reptiles." We notice that we are not talking about the events in the garden of Eden here; Paul points us back to long before then. Eve disobeyed by eating fruit from a tree, whereas Paul speaks of "images" or "idols."

When God first said, "Let us make man in our image" (Gen 1:26 KJV), we presume that the breath of God entered the hominids in question instantly, and I think we would be correct in assuming that. Jesus told us, "Flesh gives birth to flesh, but the Spirit gives birth to spirit" (John 3:6). And although we are not talking about "being born again" here, we are talking about "Spirit giving birth to spirit": to be human means to have a human spirit. Spirit is what separates us from the animal kingdom. The birth of flesh and the birth of spirit are events that happen simultaneously and quickly, (although, some mothers who have given birth may disagree with me). Birth is unlike a gradual evolution that happens over millennia, and in that respect birth happens instantaneously—birth of flesh and birth of spirit.

Yet, there is another angle we need to pursue. Once a child is born into the world the parents will start the process of encouraging the child's development by feeding their offspring nutritiously and playing with them and giving the child small jobs in order to stimulate the growth of their mind and muscles. Eventually the children will mature into fine adults. Perhaps a similar process happens with the human spirit. When God said, "Let us make man in our image, in our likeness" we can see two procedures taking place—an instant procedure when God first administered spirit to humans beings, but also an elongated process where the humans were being made in God's image through a prolonged procedure that meant the human spirit would be guided and encouraged in its growth towards being like God; similar to how we guide our children into adulthood. When we say of a baby "a man has been born into the world" we acknowledge that several years of growth must first take place. There are two facets of men being made into God's image: firstly, as individuals being made in God's image, and secondly, as a collective group maturing into God's likeness. That may be why we get the two words "image" and "likeness" in Genesis 1:26.

God helped shape the "spirit" of the human beings, by moving them forward and helping them to mature into fine spiritual adults who had God's likeness upon them. This could have taken decades for the individuals concerned. After all, I have been a Christian since I was a child, and daily I find I am still growing and that God has much to teach me. I'm sure other Christians will agree that we still have much to learn in our walk with the Lord.

So although the people in those far off early days of humanity were upright in heart, they could still be made into the similitude of God as time went by. We'll understand this a little better if we take Jesus as an example. Christ was born upright, without sin, and yet we read that "Jesus grew in wisdom and stature, and in favor with God and man" (Luke 2:52). That is a picture of early man too, though "upright" in nature, they were still being made into the likeness of God as each day passed.

> And we all, with unveiled face, beholding the glory of the Lord, are being transformed into the same image from one degree of glory to another. (2 Cor 3:18 ESV)

Collectively, as a society, the shaping of the "human spirit" into the image of God could have taken millennia as one degree of glory moved on to the next degree of glory. Each successive generation would build on the previous generation's experience resulting in each human family, group, or clan reflecting more of God's image. For God's good qualities are vast and reflecting them all is beyond the reach of an ordinary human being, although we can all reflect certain facets of God's glory.

This state of growth did not mean the people were sinful or unrighteous, far from it, but it did mean they were growing in the likeness of God. Their innocence was not diminished by reason of their "discernment" growing.

Chapter 12
The Competition

God was shaping and making man in his likeness. But, we remember, "elohim" can mean a class of beings too, so when God said, "Let us make man in our image" there seemed to be one particular elohim, traditionally known as Lucifer, who found himself irked by God's statement of intent to make man in his own image. (The Hebrew word for Lucifer means "shining one." Modern versions of the Bible translate the word as "morning star.")

Lucifer saw no competitor as God formed the animals, indeed, we are told in Job that as God marked out the earth's dimensions and laid its foundations, the "morning stars sang together and all the angels shouted for joy" (Job 38:4–7). The angels rejoiced as they saw God's handiwork progress. But God announced to them that he was going to make one of the earthly creatures in his image, and one particular angel's joy was turned into indignation. For this angel saw a competitor when the lowly man made from dirt was made in the likeness of God—the effrontery and audacity of it. Lucifer rebelled saying, "I will make myself like the Most High" (Isa 14:14).

Therefore Lucifer took pains to hinder the process of sons of dust being turned into "Elohim's" image and likeness. Could these lowly earthly creatures reflect such a high majestic glory as God's? Lucifer thought not, and made it his objective to reveal to God exactly why these mean, menial men were unworthy recipients, and to let it be known why they were unable to carry such a weight of glory. Lucifer became the "accuser" (Rev 12:10). We see a good example of this in the story of Job where God points out to Satan that Job is upright, blameless, and shuns evil. Satan responds, "Does Job fear God for nothing? Have you not put a hedge around him and his household and everything he has? You have blessed the work of his hands, so that his flocks and herds are spread throughout the land. But now stretch out your hand and strike everything he has, and he will surely curse you to your face" (Job 1:9–11).

Satan got to the task of placing serious obstacles in Job's path of righteousness, impediments that would deflect him from his upright course. This was work that Satan was familiar with. The angel whose pride had been injured when God first began the process of turning clay creatures into images of elohim—who better to carry out this task? Satan could bring much experience to bear by the time Job's testing came, he could throw some of his supreme snags, stumbling blocks, and sinful snares Job's way. Satan had been at this job of work thousands of years, and that's why in Genesis chapter 3 he is introduced to us as having a history.

> Now the serpent was more crafty than any beast of the field. (Gen 3:1)

The serpent is announced as having prior form. He has a history of craftiness. He's wily, watch out! Genesis 3:1 is a warning: the serpent has been about his scheming underhand business for a long time. God, of course, did not make him as such, he became crafty to prove his own proud point.

Meanwhile, back in Romans chapter 1, Paul gives us some insight into how Satan went about his work with early humankind. Images or idols were his first port of call. God had mentioned the word "image" when he said, "Let us make man in our image," so Satan made a point of encouraging human beings to craft images. God is Spirit, so inanimate terracotta figurines will never represent who God is. Satan may have reasoned, *the Most High wants to make clay men into his image, well then I will show him that these men can make clay into an image of him.* God told the Israelites not to make an image. Idols, icons, and images had always been, and would always be, a snare into which human beings could fall and lose their freedom. The Ubaid society that Adam and Eve lived in after they left the garden had their fair share of serpent-like figurines. Rachel carried on with the tradition stealing her father Laban's teraphim. The nation of Israel struggled with the "unclean thing" too. David sang, "I will set no thing of Belial before mine eyes" (Ps 103:3 DBT). Ezekiel's message to the Israelites was, "Turn from your idols and renounce all your detestable practices!" (Ezek 14:6). We remember how quick the emancipated Israelites were to cast a golden calf in the wilderness, only a few days after God had spoken to them regarding the command to avoid the snare of idols and other gods.

The Competition

Satan set about his work of tainting the work of God in man. The devil, as he is often called, is a spiritual being and now that humankind had spirit wedded to their biological frame Satan was able to work deep in the heart of man. Our spirit reaches a long way down to the very core of our being; our physical body has been breathed upon by God's Spirit thereby raising it higher than the brute beasts. "So we fix our eyes not on what is seen, but on what is unseen, since what is seen is temporary, but what is unseen is eternal," said Paul to the Corinthians. Our spirit is, by far, the major facet a human being possesses. Solomon gives us a little insight into just how large the spirit of a human being is compared to our physical body when he says, "Like a gold ring in a pig's snout is a beautiful woman who shows no discretion" (Prov 11:22). Notice how large the physical beauty part of the woman is—not very large at all, it's the size of a ring, but look how large the lack of discretion is, it's the size of a pig. Discretion, (or indiscretion) of course, emanates from our inner man, our invisible heart. Our invisible soul and spirit are, by a long measure, bigger and carry far more importance than our physical body.

And yet we cannot see spirit. Satan, with his malevolent intent, persuaded other spiritual beings like himself to join his cause. The dragon in the book of Revelation (12:4) swept a third of the stars out of the sky and cast them to the earth. The book of Revelation, as its name suggests, reveals to us that the serpent persuaded one third of the angelic hosts to join forces with him.

> Then war broke out in heaven. Michael and his angels fought against the dragon, and the dragon and his angels fought back. (Rev 12:7)

Together the rebellious spirits looked for ways to prove their case: that earthly man was not capable of bearing God's image. The angels who aligned themselves to Lucifer's movement lost their positions as God's holy angels and became tainted too.

Images were the first diversion tactic used by the unclean spirits. Idols and figurines were the unclean spirits' weapons of warfare in which humanity could become entangled and wounded. Men and women would naturally want to worship God, so if Satan could divert this worship he would be seizing ground.

Other temptations followed: God had directed humans in Genesis chapter 1 to "Be fruitful and increase in number," so if Satan could arrange for men and women to avoid this directive it would suit his purpose. We find that Paul highlights this straight after he has mentioned the idols. "Therefore God gave them over in the sinful desires of their hearts to sexual impurity for the degrading of their bodies with one another. They exchanged the truth about God for a lie, and worshiped and served created things rather than the Creator" (Rom 1:24-25).

Formerly lovers had been faithful to one another because their love itself sustained them and their love was only satisfied with their beloved. But the infiltration of unclean spirits mingling in the hidden depths of the human spirit meant a temptation towards unfaithfulness could then begin to surface.

Paul continues, "For this reason God gave them over to degrading passions; for their women exchanged the natural function for that which is unnatural, and in the same way also the men abandoned the natural function of the woman and burned in their desire toward one another, men with men committing indecent acts and receiving in their own persons the due penalty of their error" (26-27 NASB). Paul doesn't mention exactly what the shameful acts were, apart from mentioning they were "shameful." Paul told the Ephesians, "It is shameful even to mention what the disobedient do in secret" (Eph 5:12).

Paul continues, "And just as they did not see fit to acknowledge God any longer, God gave them over to a depraved mind, to do those things which are not proper, being filled with all unrighteousness, wickedness, greed, evil; full of envy, murder, strife, deceit, malice; they are gossips, slanderers, haters of God, insolent, arrogant, boastful, inventors of evil, disobedient to parents, without understanding, untrustworthy, unloving, unmerciful" (Rom 1:28-31).

Three times, in Romans chapter 1, we read the phrase, "Therefore God gave them over." In shaping humanity into his own image God needed pliable clay to work with, and that is the problem working with creatures that have freewill. Freewill would not be freewill if the creatures were forced into being compliant. God was willing to impress his image deep within us but we were being uncooperative.

"Therefore God gave them over in the sinful desires of their hearts" (24). That's our fallen nature; we have been "given over" to our sinful desires. The serpent managed to inject his poison into the spiritual makeup of humankind. We don't know how many humans were on the earth when this happened, but the sinfulness within us spread across people and then into successive generations around the globe. As the King James Bible reminds us, "A little leaven leaveneth the whole lump" (Gal 5:9). God lifted his hands and allowed us to chart our own course; he gave us over to our own devices. "God has locked all people in the prison of their own disobedience" (Rom 11:32 ISV).

Moses points the new nation of Israel (and us) back to the time of the fall of humanity when he proclaims in Deuteronomy 32:7, "Remember the days of old; consider the generations long past." In verse 5 (KJV) he says, "They have corrupted themselves, their spot *is not* the spot of his children: *they are* a perverse and crooked generation." He continues, "Their wine is the venom of serpents, the deadly poison of cobras" (33 NIV). Satan infiltrated humankind's spiritual territory and injected us with his poison, our spirits were tainted, we had a "spot" and a "blemish." God had been willing to work with us but because of our insistence to follow another route he "gave us over." We can imagine the LORD saying, "Alright then, if that is what you want, I cannot contend with you forever." We get another picture of this when we move into Genesis 6:3, which highlights God's heart: "Then the LORD said, 'My Spirit will not contend with humans forever.'" The text is not here talking about what happened at the original fall, but it is an intimate revealing of God's heart and how he would have felt towards the earlier human beings.

If a hairdresser is cutting my hair and I keep moving around in the chair, at some point the hairdresser will ask me to be still. If I persist, the hairdresser will cease to cut my hair and I will be left for my hair to develop its own bird's nest state, as well as incurring the wrath of the hairdresser. Me walking around with messy hair would be nobody's fault but mine. The scriptures paint the picture of the human race getting too unwieldy for God to handle so "he gave them over." Not because God was too weak, but for reason that he was working with precision and the delicate nature of the proceedings required a stillness from the subjects, if the subjects became unruly and wild as he tried to complete his good work, then the subjects of his craftsmanship would become objects of his wrath. (Sometimes parents of unruly children do the same.)

Now we all have the spot, every last one of us. We are born with it. We may notice that from our earliest years something is not quite aligned within us, there is a blemish, a hankering after, a pursuit that's not productive. We also find a willingness to stand proud, causing us to point the finger, and all sorts of other unhelpful maladies. Our spiritual DNA has been infected. We are no use for God's original intent. The rebellious angel is beginning to look as if he was correct. In fact, as far as God is concerned, we are dead and lost.

Jesus explained to the disciples that it was not what went into a man's mouth that defiled him but what came out. "Don't you see that whatever enters the mouth goes into the stomach and then out of the body? But the things that come out of a person's mouth come from the heart, and these defile them. For out of the heart come evil thoughts—murder, adultery, sexual immorality, theft, false testimony, slander. These are what defile a person" (Matt 15:17–20). Our hearts are defiled, they have a blemish and the blemish works its way through the whole man. James said that a "person is tempted when they are dragged away by their own evil desire and enticed. Then, after desire has conceived, it gives birth to sin; and sin, when it is full-grown, gives birth to death" (Jas 1:14–15). The blemish in our heart will work its way through us until its corruption is complete.

> This is what the Lord says: "Your wound is incurable, your injury beyond healing. There is no one to plead your cause, no remedy for your sore, no healing for you." (Jer 30:12–13)

There is no healing for this wound, it is incurable. Has God lost this battle with his adversary "the serpent"?

Chapter 13
Creation Groans

*The whole creation has been groaning as in the pains of childbirth
right up to the present time.* (Rom 8:22)

THE DOCTRINE OF THE fall is basic "reaping what we sow." God uses the physical world as a reflection of our spiritual state. He teaches us spiritual truths through the mirror of the material world. (I explore this theme in my book *Fishing for Praise*.) The present universe reveals that all is not well, which includes the state of the human soul. We see that man is born to trouble, we are reaping what we have sown, but by God's good grace the trouble can teach us important lessons.

We are presently living in what John in the book of Revelation calls the "old order of things" (21:4). At this present time, evil is in the world and creation groans under the weight of reflecting that fact. The universe is predisposed to react negatively to evil; God created it that way. God saw that all he had made was "very good" and an inbuilt alarm was an element of that goodness—if humans were to take an evil course, creation would alert us that something was amiss. Part of the message in Romans chapter 8 is that creation groans under the weight of evil that's done.

Let's remember, that even before humans had made room for sin, God did not make the world free from sharp corners where humans could hurt themselves, there are cliffs that a person may fall from, there are accidents waiting to happen. Incumbent upon us is the duty to use our reason to negotiate difficult situations carefully or we may get injured, or injure someone else. The first humans, though upright in nature, could get hurt just as we can get hurt. Responsibility is given us as a component of being made in God's image. Let's say someone is cutting down a tall tree but doesn't bother to warn anyone and someone gets injured when the tree falls. Negligent behavior can result in someone being hurt—a person's fallen nature has caused injury to another. Or deceit may hurt people who thought they could trust each other, relationships fail because of infidelity and deception. The tangled web we weave leaves a trail of pain in its wake. So in that sense, human sin has made the world a more treacherous place to live.

We also need to consider microorganisms that can spread among humans. An explosion of bacteria may occur, sometimes caused by human behavior that facilitates a disease through unhygienic practices, and at other times we may not be certain what brings a disease among us. Or an earthquake may devastate an area. Plus war, criminal behavior, and hundreds of other things go wrong that stop life on earth from being as God wills. All of the trouble in the world cannot be attributed to human agencies but some of it can and God allows other calamities for his own reasons.

The danger in the universe alerts us to the fact that "humans with spirit" are not in a settled environment yet. The hazards and trouble show us that this universe is temporary. The struggle also allows us to see that we need help in our quest to grow in the image and likeness of God. Peril can be what C. S. Lewis called a "severe mercy." We see things go wrong, and sometimes disastrously wrong, consequently our illusory "self-sufficiency" is seen to be fallacious and we are warned of our need.

As we move from 50,000 BC, or what we know as the Upper Paleolithic Period (late stages of the Old Stone Age) towards 20,000 to 10,000 BC, or what we know as the Mesolithic Period (Middle Stone Age) we find, archaeologically, that tools are varied and the beginnings of animal domesticity has begun—the first dog buried together with a human is found in Palestine and is dated 12,000 years ago. We also find human settlements near rivers during the Mesolithic Period. The dispersal of humans out of Africa would naturally slow down because there is only so much earth to fill, but that doesn't mean the humans should stop their journeying lifestyle. Routes, tracks, and trails could still be explored even though the main migration had taken place. God would continue to supply the needs of the people if their trust was placed in him—their life of faith in God's providing hand would continue. But "when the Son of Man comes, will he find faith on the earth?" (Luke 18:8). Faith in God could grow or diminish depending on the developmental growth of human beings into the image of God.

Many temptations dogged the way. One of which may have been what Yuval Noah Harari calls "the luxury trap."

"But wouldn't it be easier . . . ," we can almost hear the luxury trap begin to beckon, "if food could be grown in one area alone, and then you could take life easy with no more traveling around looking for food sources and worrying about where your next meal will be coming from?"

The end of the Mesolithic Period gave rise to the Neolithic Period (New Stone Age). This juncture also flags the end of the Ice Age (Pleistocene Epoch), when the ice caps began to recede and the temperature raised a few degrees.

The timing for the changeover of "ages" was not exact and took place at different times for different regions on the planet. Genesis chapter 2 leads us into the Neolithic Period that originally began in the Near East at roughly 10,000 BC. But Genesis chapter 2 picks up the story in the years around 5500 BC. This period was an important phase of human development and also an era of God speaking to men. God stayed close at hand despite human beings giving up the lifestyle that he had originally intended for them. Men wanted to settle down—no more foraging or twenty-mile hunting trips—so they chose Harari's luxury trap and began their static subsistence.

We get the feel that God is not pleased with the new step being taken by humankind at this juncture of history; the schemes Solomon informed us about may have been well underway by this time. The word "schemes" in Hebrew does not necessarily infer sinfulness; the word can mean "inventions" or "devices." Satan's schemes are often means of conflict for human beings. He introduces us to rancor, animosity, jealousy, greed, etc., but at other times he may simply use inventions or schemes that seem like a good idea at the time. When we follow these "good ideas" we may be waylaid from our original path and find that we have lost something we had and can't get it back. As the old song says, "He got what he wanted, but he lost what he had."[1]

Hunter-gatherer diets were healthy and nutritious. Their fare included a wide variety of plants, roots, tubers, vegetables, nuts, berries, fruit, meat, and fish. Starvation wasn't an issue in places with multiple food sources. Men enjoyed the camaraderie of being in a hunting party. They ran long distances and used the wits and dominating skills that God had given them to overcome animals. Women enjoyed the socializing aspect of being with

---

1. Little Richard, "He Got What He Wanted," 1962.

other women as they gathered fruits and vegetables, trapped small animals, and became adept at cooking food—cooked food requires less calories for people to digest it, a useful quality in those days. The women folk (and any men who were interested) would have shared tips about preparing food, much like we see on TV today. Children would have played around the women, or stayed in camp with their elderly relatives. Women who had no children could join the men on their outings.

But after millennia of the simple life people decided they wanted to experiment with growing mass food sources in one location. The initial stages of the "working week" were put into place—the first settlers could not simply plant seeds and expect all to be well. The land first needed to be cleared and plowed, and the sprouting plants would need to be protected from birds that may devour them and other animals that may trample them. The ground would need to be kept free of competing indigenous plants vying for the same patch of land. Water would also need to be directed to the plants and the irrigation channels kept free from the build up of silt. British archaeologist Diana Kirkbride states, "Although the plants were to become the slaves of men, men were equally to become the serfs of the plants, and the same applies to animal domestication."[2]

We admire the skill involved in slowly cultivating crops, but as the initial agriculturalists became dependent on their cultivated crops their food intake became nutritionally restrictive. Hunter-gatherers ate a diverse diet and got plenty of exercise, while sedentary farming communities stayed in one location and ate limited nutritional sources. Clark Spencer Larsen, a biological anthropologist at Ohio State University, suggests that the first agricultural revolution, also known as the Neolithic Revolution, was not an upturn of events for human beings. Eating the same domesticated grain daily gave early farmers tooth cavities and gum disease that were rarely found in hunter-gatherers. The newly domesticated cattle, sheep, and goats may have become sources of milk and meat but they were also a source of parasites and new infectious diseases. Early farmers suffered from iron deficiency and developmental delays, and they shrank in stature.[3]

There were eight basic plant species around Mesopotamia that were domesticated into what became the first large scale agricultural projects known to humans—three cereals, four legumes (or pulses), and flax. These plants were developed in the Fertile Crescent, and that is where we see the

---

2. Kirkbride, "Umm Dabaghiyah," 11.
3. Gibbons, "Evolution of Diet," 51.

civilized world beginning to take shape—life as we know it today. Although it happened over 7,000 years ago this period was the beginnings of the modern life we live today. The first strains of the settled lifestyle went back even further to 9000 or 10,000 BC, when men first began to experiment with crops. Slowly, sedentary farming began to gain momentum over the itinerant traveling nomadic lifestyle.

We call those early days of agriculture and civilization "progress," and they were, but when we read Genesis and other parts of the Bible we get the feeling that, although we label this crossroads in history as progress, it was not the sort of advancement that God wanted human beings to make. There was nothing inherently wrong about this advancement but for many thousands of years humankind had lived another way. Suddenly, relatively speaking, all was about to change. I am not in a position to judge how life would have turned out if humans had continued to live naturally off the land, with their own camps and fireside fellowship, but many of the problems we have today may not have arisen at all if we had continued along that route. Modern humans have lived an uncomplicated lifestyle for 193,000 years, but for the last 7,000 years we have made life far more complex. If we look on those figures as a chart we see that humans lived simply for 96.5 percent of their existence on the planet but for the last 3.5 percent we have cluttered the earth with our attempts at affluence and byproducts of luxurious living. In some ways we can look at the progress of the last 7,000 years as an improvement and in other ways it can be viewed as a move in the wrong direction. As the singer/songwriter Larry Norman wrote, "Sometimes I think that we've advanced but then I look at where we are."[4]

We immediately question how all the world's people would get food if we didn't live in the sophisticated way we do nowadays. And that is a valid point, but perhaps we have made our own population problems—with the invention of agriculture, human females began to bear babies in rapid succession.[5] Looking back at recent and not-so-recent civilized history we see that many of the world's people did not have access to a plentiful food supply. Even today undernourished people are a problem in developing countries; wealthy nations too have their share of people who have access to food but can still be suffering from malnutrition because of the type of food they eat. Perhaps if we had stayed on the route of the first 193,000 years the

4. Norman, "Déjà vu," 1976.
5. Gibbons, "Evolution of Diet," 50.

world would have taken longer to populate, but the air would be cleaner, the land would be uncluttered, and there would be peace in the valley.

The nutrition that early agriculturally cultivated crops consisted of did not yield the full compliment of vitamins, minerals, and protein that had been a feature of our former lifestyle. Highly domesticated strains of wheat cannot survive in the wild. Personally, I love to eat bread but perhaps it is not quite as natural as I would like to think. Hunter-gatherer skeletons reveal them to be healthier than the people who ate agricultural crop produce, with a stronger bone density.[6] The Hunter-gatherers' general health seems to have been robust, they were taller than the sedentary agriculturalists, had fewer signs of tooth decay, lower rates of arthritis, and iron deficiency was not a problem because of the varied diet hunted and gathered before the domesticated era that began some 7,000 years ago.[7] Furthermore in today's world our brains appear to be smaller and farming is in the frame as the reason why. Scientists estimate that the downturn has occurred within the last 10,000 years of human history. Agriculture, restricted diets, and urbanization are thought to be the reason.[8]

Micah, in the Bible, mentions a time when men "will beat their swords into plowshares and their spears into pruning hooks. Nation will not take up sword against nation, nor will they train for war anymore. Everyone will sit under their own vine and under their own fig tree" (4:3–4). These verses point us to a time when life will be significantly less intricate, and humans will be satisfied with what they have, and be content to simply be themselves with no diversionary appendages stuck to them. Micah's words also seem to hearken back to a time when God first endowed human beings with his image; when men would make camp around a group of fruit trees that were in season and share with other groups what they had found. Zechariah also says, "In that day each of you will invite your neighbor to sit under your vine and fig tree" (3:10).

Jesus often instructs us to move back to those days where a life of simple trust in God was lived—"Give us this day our daily bread" (Matt 6:11 KJV) doesn't sound like there is much hoarding of food taking place. Jesus warned us about the man who said, "This is what I'll do. I will tear down my

---

6. Ryan and Shaw, "Graciality," lines 1–2, 18–20.

7. Elliemaeh, "Hunting and Gathering: The Healthiest Human Diet," A Mom on a Mission . . . to Nurture and Nourish Her Family (blog), March 16, 2011, para. 1. https://amomonamission.wordpress.com/2011/03/16/hunting-and-gathering-the-healthiest-human-diet/.

8. Macrae, "Getting Smaller," lines 13–16.

barns and build bigger ones, and there I will store my surplus grain" (Luke 12:18). Jesus directs us to another way of life. Modern, or what we call "civilized" life does not seem to sit well with Jesus. He also said, "Therefore I tell you, do not worry about your life, what you will eat or drink; or about your body, what you will wear. Is not life more than food, and the body more than clothes? Look at the birds of the air; they do not sow or reap or store away in barns, and yet your heavenly Father feeds them. Are you not much more valuable than they?" (Matt 6:25–26).

The Old Testament also speaks of those simpler times. "The Lord is my shepherd, I lack nothing. He makes me lie down in green pastures, he leads me beside quiet waters, he refreshes my soul" (Ps 23:1–3).

God gave men freewill as a gift and we can use it as we will. But sometimes children move in a direction their parents would rather not see them go. Such seems to be the situation with humanity as we moved into the domesticated age. But even so, God moved and worked with us, he is not going to abandon us or leave us to our own devices without help and he continues his first pursuit of making humankind into his image and likeness.

The restrictive diet of the Mesopotamian agriculturalists took its toll on those who chose it and also began to coerce human evolution into an area that nature had not intended. A cereal is a grass that has been cultivated for its edible components, which is what we know as grain. Animals are designed to eat grass: cattle, goats, sheep, and other ruminant animals have the enzymes, acids, and microbes in their four stomachs that are able to digest the cellulose in the green grass blades. We remember that in Genesis 1:30 God gave the "green plants" to the animals. We humans, on the other hand, can't eat regular grass. However, we can eat certain components of grass. We can eat the grain if we treat it. We are all familiar with grass family members such as wheat, barley, corn, rice, oats, rye, and millet. But because grains are designed to endure, we can't digest them raw. Grains should really be flaked, cracked, puffed, popped, or ground before being consumed. In the course of time we noticed that whole grains tend to go rancid faster than refined versions due to their fat content. Milling the bran and the germ away gives the cereal (what we know as) a longer shelf life. So, making food cultivation a little more complicated, food processing started preserving grain by stripping away the advantageous bran and germ.

Other crops produced in the early days of agriculture were legumes or pulses. The term "legume" refers to plants whose fruit is enclosed in a pod. Pulses are part of the legume family, but the term "pulse" refers only to the dried seed. Dried peas, edible beans, lentils, and chickpeas are the most common varieties of pulses. These seeds have a strong outer layer because they may need to stay in the soil for a long while until the conditions for them to germinate are right. Their tough exterior protects them from the weather, insects, and bacteria. That's why we need to soak beans and help remove the phytic acid and lectin that protect them. The strong substances that protect the seed can adversely affect humans. We know that Paleolithic man did eat some legumes, along with all his other food, but a problem may occur when all we eat is cereals and legumes—a situation that could have existed in the Neolithic era.

Several unintended byproducts of exchanging the itinerant lifestyle for a sedentary lifestyle ensued, one of which was "money." We see early exchanges of an economic kind taking place in the Neolithic Period. Excavations have brought to light remains of textiles, flint, stone, pottery, wooden vessels, and salt used for trading purposes. Those people who lead a nomadic lifestyle did not seem to eat salt with their meals.[9] As civilization began to take shape and salt-rich game was exchanged for a Neolithic menu of cultivated crops, salt was now needed as a supplement. The people of the Paleolithic era did not appear to add salt to their food. Evidence for sea or brine salt extraction or mining for salt by prehistoric people does not seem to exist. Carnivores, including humans, obtain enough salt from meat and seafood. The picture changes when developed crops became the main food source. Domesticated animals were also a part of the Neolithic agricultural revolution, but even so, "salt" became a valuable resource for civilized communities.

Cakes of salt have been used as money in later times too. The Latin word for "salt" has evolved into our modern word "salary." Soldiers were sometimes paid in salt. A person who does their work well is said to be "worth their salt."

Money is another product that God doesn't seem too happy about. We get the impression that Jesus didn't carry much money with him, and on one occasion had to ask for someone to lend him a coin. "Bring me a denarius and let me look at it" (Mark 12:15). When Jesus sent out his 12 apostles his message to them was, "Do not get any gold or silver or copper to take with you in your belts" (Matt 10:9). When Jesus instructs his 72 disciples how to execute their mission his first rule was "Do not take a purse" (Luke 10:4). When Peter and Jesus paid the temple tax, Peter was told to use

---

9. Wood et al., "Salt (NaCl)," lines 32–35.

his fishing line to catch a fish that had providentially eaten a four-drachma coin, because apparently there wasn't any money in the house. "But so that we may not cause offense, go to the lake and throw out your line. Take the first fish you catch; open its mouth and you will find a four-drachma coin. Take it and give it to them for my tax and yours" (Matt 17:27). We also notice that Jesus paid the tax only as a concession.

Modern life is predominantly based upon our economy, and God graciously works with us and helps provide for our needs. Reading through the scriptures, money seems to be tolerated but not celebrated. The Apostle Paul suggests setting aside a sum of money each week to the churches in Corinth and Galatia and most modern church services include "tithes and offerings" as a part of their service. We preface our giving with statements such as, "Let us bring our offerings to the Lord," but in reality, "every animal of the forest is mine, and the cattle on a thousand hills" (Ps 50:10). God has no need of our money and can find other methods of supplying our needs. We accommodate money because the global arrangement warrants it. The modern metaphorical statement "a necessary evil" may be too strong a phrase but "lucre" probably falls into one of the "schemes" that Solomon said led humanity off course, especially when it becomes "filthy lucre." We know the "love of money" is a dangerous root, and while money itself may not be evil, the alluring honey trap it lays before each one of us makes praying "lead me not into temptation" a priority for us all.

Chapter 14

The Center of Civilization

Living in one location requires a consistent supply of fresh water, and that is why the Fertile Crescent made such an ideal location for domestic development. The main rivers in the crescent were:

- The Nile, giving rise to the Egyptian community (if we include Egypt in the Fertile Crescent).
- The Jordan where the people of Jericho and other settlements were based.
- The Euphrates and the Tigris—the land between them was called Mesopotamia.
- The Pishon (mentioned in Genesis). This river dried up but looks like it flowed northwards from the Arabian Peninsula into southern Mesopotamia and then emptied into the Persian Gulf along with the Euphrates and the Tigris.
- The Gihon (also mentioned in Genesis and also dried up). Most Bibles translate the river Gihon as winding through the land of Cush. Ham fathered Cush, and Cush was the father of Nimrod. Nimrod ruled in Mesopotamia (Gen 10:6–12). It's likely that Cush gave his name (Sumerian "Kish") to a city and to the area that the river ran through.
- The Balikh is a tributary of the Euphrates and has its source just south of Haran, the northern town where Abraham made his first stopping point after leaving the city of Ur.
- The Khabur originates in Turkey and joins the Euphrates in Syria. First Chronicles 5:26 states that when the Reubenites, the Gadites, and

the half tribe of Manasseh were taken into exile they went to Habor (Khabur) where there was a river. The Khabur river was sometimes identified with the Chebar river that is mentioned in the first verse of the first chapter of Ezekiel. But modern scholars identify Ezekiel's Chebar river as a canal toward the east of Babylon. And some Bibles translate it that way: "I was among the exiles by the Chebar canal" (Ezek 1:1 ESV).

Rivers were important for navigation as well as fresh water. When Jacob journeyed north en route to meet his wife Rachel, the second half of his journey would mean following the Euphrates northwest toward the Balikh river and then walking beside the Balikh northwards until he reached the vicinity of Haran.

There were of course other settlements around the world. Anatolia is based at the intersection of Asia and Europe, and located northwest of Mesopotamia. In Anatolia during the seventh millennium BC we see the beginnings of farming, including crop husbandry, but it is southern Mesopotamia, lying to the southeast of Anatolia and situated between the Tigris and Euphrates rivers that is the focus of Genesis chapters 2–11.

God's agenda for human beings did not appear to include forsaking the simple life, but leave it we did, and proceeded to create local environments where people no longer needed to be mobile. Formerly, humans had traversed the landscape to where seasonal food would naturally grow, but relatively suddenly, in what is known as the "Neolithic Revolution," lifestyles changed dramatically. And although God may not have intended this agriculturally based sedentary way of life for human beings, he was willing to work with us. God created us to be the recipients of his love. He won't be moved in his objective to love us even if we follow our own paths.

> And so we know and rely on the love God has for us. God is love.
> (1 John 4:16)

During the transition period Mesopotamian farmers were experimenting with crops and slowly cultivating domestic cereals and pulses. Crops such as wheat, barley, lentils, and peas have a quick turnaround period between planting and harvesting, usually a matter of months. Fruit trees, however, need a longer investment period before fruit can be harvested. Early farmers would be reticent to cultivate fruit trees that needed years of care and attention before they would bear viable fruit. Genesis chapter 2 tells us that Yahweh invested time and effort into planting a garden—if the

God and Primordial People

people would no longer go and find fruit trees that were in season, then he would help to supplement their diet by bringing fruit trees to them, thus supplying some important nutrients found in fruit. So, armed with a plan and a willingness to reach out to human beings, the Lord God took part, to some extent, in the domestication process, although he stopped short of cultivating grasses. "The Lord God had planted a garden in the east, in Eden; ... The Lord God made all kinds of trees grow" (Gen 2:8–9). The fruit trees that were planted in the garden began as seeds originating in other parts of the globe and thereby the Lord God played a small part in the Neolithic Revolution. In a similar way Jesus fed the 5,000 and 4,000 people with bread, and bread is a product of grass which needs specific cultivation—years of sowing the correct types of grain by singling out the larger grains and sowing them again and so on annually until a grass yielded a useful head of grain. Yes, God works with us but he is ready to point out that we have left the original pathway that we were designed to travel. Jesus seemed to point to the time of the Neolithic Revolution, which began the process of sowing, reaping, and storing, when he said,

> Look at the birds of the air; they do not sow or reap or store away in barns, and yet your heavenly Father feeds them. (Matt 6:26)

Birds and animals have their migratory pathways through the earth. God had a pathway for human beings too, both literally and figuratively, but leaving the pathway incurred ensuing temptations along the way. We ought to mention that a good percentage of the grain that was stored away in Neolithic silos was used for ale. Once the procedure of grains being ground into flour to make bread had been perfected, some Neolithic farmers found that grains could also be malted, mashed, and fermented resulting in a beverage we know as ale. The Sumerians used roughly 40 percent of the locally produced grain for ale.[1]

Genesis 2:6 says, "streams came up from the earth and watered the whole surface of the ground," informing us that water was used to help with irrigation. Modern historians say the area of southern Mesopotamia became populated around 5500 BC, although some small communities located there a little earlier. The archaeological levels at Eridu suggest 5400 BC as the time when the first settlers' reed houses were erected. Irrigation played a major part in the agricultural revolution.

---

1. Goucher and Walton, *World History*, 39–40.

The Center of Civilization

Northern Mesopotamia had been the site of settled communities long before southern Mesopotamia. Archaeologists date settlements in northern Mesopotamia at around 9000 BC, and call this period the "Pre-Pottery Neolithic A," with the period's main features being circular mud brick dwellings and the cultivation of crops.

The following period is called the "Pre-Pottery Neolithic B," ranging from approximately 7500 BC to 6000 BC. In this time period flint tools are in evidence and the domestication of animals seems to have played a larger part. The animals (beasts of burden) would be able to help with land cultivation or could be used for food. The architecture of buildings in this period moved away from being round to "boat shaped." In the Levant, the buildings had straight lines. A heavy helping of highly polished lime plaster was laid down as flooring in the houses.

We have four names for the next period because four cultures have qualities distinct from each other but belong roughly in the same time period:

1. The Hassuna culture was based in northern Mesopotamia around 6000 BC. A farming community that created its own fine pottery that replaced earlier inelegant pottery. The pots of this period were often cream-colored slip with reddish paint in linear designs. ("Slip" means the pot had an extra fine layer adding smoothness to the finish and helping to make the pot watertight.) The Hassuna people had their own pottery kilns capable of remarkably high firing temperatures.[2] A feature of the culture's modern conveniences included grain grinders, baking ovens and bins, as well as a good compliment of tools.

2. The Samarra culture, which got underway slightly after the Hassuna culture, was known for its prosperously settled and highly organized social structure, as well as its own brand of finely made pottery. The Samarran pottery was fired to a higher temperature than had previously been used, reaching temperatures of 1100 degrees C.[3]

3. The Halaf culture, running concurrently with the Hassuna and Samarra cultures, was located in what are now southeast Turkey, Syria, and northern Iraq. Halaf pottery was state of the art, fired in double-chamber kilns, with detailed artistic geometric designs painted in varying colors. Skilled men and women, known as "potters," appear to have made Halaf ware. Halaf ceramics found their way far and wide,

2. Streily, "Early Pottery," 73.
3. Ibid.

including to Iran, probably because of its fine quality, durability, and pleasing form.

4. The Ubaid culture takes us down to southern Mesopotamia. This is the era that we are interested in as students of the Bible because Genesis chapter 2 points us in that direction.

Southern Mesopotamia had not been a popular place to settle, unlike northern Mesopotamia and the Levant. Genesis 2 relays that "there was no man to cultivate the ground," and the simple reason was that vegetation was scarce; the area was basically arid. But around 6000 to 5000 BC things began to change—fresh water arrived in abundance. This environmental development could have been partly from natural climatic change, because at that time the most recent Ice Age had ended and the present Holocene Epoch had got well underway, giving the waterways a boost with more rain falling in the Taurus Mountains in eastern Turkey, allowing the Tigris and Euphrates rivers an increase in volume. The two other rivers, the Pishon and the Gihon also helped to supply southern Mesopotamia with water. Archaeologists have suggested that a complex system of freshwater supplies were found in southern Mesopotamia sometime after 6500 BC.[4] The area has changed again since those days, but in the era we are speaking of a profusion of fresh water found its way to southern Mesopotamia.

Once fresh water started to arrive in copious amounts, people were not slow to follow and soon started to settle in the same area of southern Mesopotamia. The possibility of crops being planted presented itself to enterprising people, and the first settlement for newly arrived human beings in southern Mesopotamia is called Oueili (Awayli). Around 6000 BC the first settlers started to occupy Oueili, according to the British Museum. The settlement at Oueili was the first community in the Ubaid period in southern Mesopotamia—technically called "Ubaid 0." The people of Oueili would be ready to work and utilize the groundwater for barley by digging irrigation channels connected to nearby rivers, streams, and freshwater lakes and marshes.

The second Ubaid settlement to spring up is known as Eridu. Professor Fuad Safar, the celebrated Iraqi archaeologist, found the remains of a canal running through Eridu. Genesis chapter 2 relates that the four rivers converged in that area. Eridu, and what would later become the city of Ur, were close to the converging rivers.

4. Zarins, Review of *Early History*, 57.

The Center of Civilization

In written records, the people of Sumer credit Enki for the arrival of water. Enki means "Lord of the earth" and also "Lord of freshwater." The Sumerian people located in southern Mesopotamia used "En" as a prefix and both Seth and Cain gave the prefix to their firstborn sons, Enosh and Enoch.

Another people group who appeared later in southern Mesopotamia were the Akkadians, and their name for Enki was "Ea," a name that the early Hebrews would identify with because the Akkadians and the Hebrews had Semitic roots. The Akkadian language and the early Hebrew language were similar. When the voice in the burning bush told Moses to "say to the Israelites: 'I am has sent me to you,'" the Hebrew word for "I am" sounded much the same as the Akkadian Ea.[5]

We think of Semitic languages starting with Noah's son Shem, from whom the title receives its name, but Shem would have spoken the same language that he was taught by his father and Noah would have spoken the language taught by his father, Lamech, and so on back in time. So in that sense the Semitic language-base goes back into prehistory.

The first expressions of writing started sometime before 3000 BC, and we call events before the dawn of writing, "prehistoric," and Proto-Semitic language does seem to go back before then. So the name of Ea would be familiar to the people in southern Mesopotamia, perhaps going back into the fifth millennium BC. "At that time people began to call on the name of the LORD" (YHWH OR YAHWEH OR YAH OR "EA" PRONOUNCED "Eyah" in a similar way to "Yah.") (Gen 4:26). But people calling on Yah or Ea did not happen until after Seth's son Enosh was born, so the life of Enosh seems to be the timeframe for the name of Ea or Yah becoming more widely known in and around the communities of southern Mesopotamia.

The fruit we know as "dates" have been found at both Oueili and Eridu.[6] While investigating the Ubaid horizon at Eridu archaeologist Seton Lloyd remarked that "buckets of date stones" were discovered there.[7] Uncultivated date palm trees grew in Egypt, Israel, Iran, and Pakistan in 6000 to 7000 BC. Some date palm trees grew wild 300 miles north of Oueili and Eridu in the Zargos mountain range but if someone wanted fresh dates to

---

5. The Hebrews would be familiar with the word Ea—the Hebrew Eyah (I am) sounds similar to the pronunciation of the Akkadian Ea. Ea's Semitic stem ḥayy means "living," the word is Old Akkadian. "Yahweh" is third person "I am," i.e., "He is," and derived from the Semitic stem hāyâ, meaning "to be."

6. Potts, *Mesopotamian Civilization*, 70.

7. Zohary et al., *Domestication of Plants*, 34.

God and Primordial People

eat in southern Mesopotamia the seeds would need to be planted manually and cared for. Gardens in southern Mesopotamia, as a general rule, would be layered, with the palm trees being the tallest, then middle and smaller trees like fig, apple, or pomegranate would grow in the shade of the palm leaves. A title for these types of gardens is "shade-tree" as the canopy provided by the taller trees contributed to a moisture rich and cooler atmosphere for the trees growing beneath, which the Mesopotamians considered to be a highly efficient system for gardens.[8] When the advent of writing began we find out that the Sumerians and Akkadians had words for pomegranates, figs, apples, grapes, plums, pears, and a mix of berries.[9] The first people to arrive in Oueili and Eridu needed a quick yield from any planting they undertook so it's unlikely the first few generations took time to plant productive fruit orchards. The palm tree is well suited to the Lower Mesopotamian alluvium but the other fruit trees would take work and need fertilizing and general care and attention.

Inscriptions written about the grove of trees at Eridu were written long after the trees themselves existed. If writing began around 3000 BC and the fruit trees were first planted sometime between 6000 and 5000 BC then up to 3,000 years could have elapsed during that time. The stories may have been embellished and changed over time before they could be recorded. The Bible claims to be the preserved record of truth, a job given by God to the children of Abraham, and before that the children of Adam, a job they have done well. The cuneiform clay tablets written by Sumerians and Akkadians, in their respective languages, can also be of interest. The "grove of Eridu" in Babylonian inscriptions called "the holy grove of Eridu" in which grew the sacred tree of life—a tree that was guarded by winged genii[10]—helps us understand that people in the same area thousands of years later understood that there was a grove of trees based close to Eridu and felt compelled to commit that story to writing. The Bible plainly remarks, "Now the LORD God had planted a garden in the east, in Eden" (Gen 2:8). The planting of the garden happened after the arrival of the water because formerly "no shrub had yet appeared on the earth and no plant had yet sprung up" (5).

There are two ways the surrounding people who lived in Oueili and Eridu could have obtained local dates to eat. The first is that they saw the

---

8. McIntosh, *Ancient Mesopotamia*, 121.
9. Potts, *Mesopotamian Civilization*, 70.
10. Norton, *Handbook of Assyriology*, s.v. "Garden of Eden," 74.

garden that had been planted by the Lord God and decided to have a go at planting a few date palms themselves. The second way is that the Lord God was happy to share his produce with the local people.

The Lord God was not simply helping supply a nutritional need with some fruit, but rather he was implementing the beginnings of an important plan. The artist, the Lord God, "Yahweh" had begun to paint a picture, he had started to act out a drama that would speak to the rest of humanity for thousands of years yet to come. But this was not simply a drama that would teach people a valuable lesson; the inception of an event that would rescue humanity from its "spot" and "blemish" had begun. Paul explains to us in Romans chapters 7 and 8 that the "law of sin and death" resides within us, leaving us "weakened by the flesh" and unable to comply to the law of God.

Verse 6 of Genesis chapter 2 notes the arrival of water, the following verse goes on to say, "Then the Lord God formed a man from the dust of the ground." We do well to remember that biblical Hebrew doesn't have a pluperfect tense. Some people are happy to point out what appears to them as an inconsistency saying, "Genesis chapter 1 has the animals created before humans but Genesis chapter 2 has a human created before the animals!" But that objection disappears once we take into account the absence of the pluperfect tense in Hebrew. The Hebrew text reads much the same as the King James Bible: "And the Lord God formed man *of* the dust of the ground." When some modern translations begin the verse with, "Then the Lord God formed man . . . ," we get the impression the event happened immediately after the arrival of the water, but that is not the case when the "Then" is removed.

We read in Genesis chapter 2:7 (KJV), "And the Lord God formed man of the dust of the ground." The meaning is, "The Lord God, who had previously formed man of the dust . . . ," which is exactly the same as Genesis 2:19 that says, "And out of the ground the Lord God formed every beast of the field, and every fowl of the air; and brought them unto Adam to see what he would call them." The meaning being that the Lord God had previously formed the beasts, which we read about in Genesis 1.

In modern English we are able to use the pluperfect tense easily. The pluperfect tense is used to indicate that an action took place before some other action in the past. We use the pluperfect tense when we use the word "had" twice in succession: "Michael arrived smelly at the party last Saturday night because he had had to retrieve his wallet that had fallen into a drain." There are other ways of using the pluperfect tense: "By the time I made

God and Primordial People

my entrance into the party Michael had left." Genesis finds another way of helping us understand the text and that is by believing what is written. If we are looking for faults (using our modern writing techniques perfected by centuries of punctuation) we can find them. But if we believe what Genesis relates, then everything falls neatly into place because "context" makes the story plain. The animals had already been created in chapter 1 before the man was created so we must be using the pluperfect tense when the animals are spoken of in chapter 2. The writer of Genesis is expecting us to put our own mind into gear when we read his words.

Genesis chapter 2 naturally follows chapter 1 chronologically, once we grasp that then the events described in Genesis fall into place historically, scientifically, geographically, and theologically.

Genesis 2:7 reminds us that, yes, God had made men (Adam plural) from the dust of the ground just as he had made the beasts. We then begin to hear about one particular man (Adam singular) whom God takes, or travels with, to the garden he had planted.

I said earlier that there is another way to view the forming of the man in Genesis 2; what takes place in the garden of Eden has layers to its narrative. When we read in chapter 2 that the LORD God formed man from the dust of the ground, we can view it in three complimentary ways—yes, we read in Genesis 1 that God did originally cause the land to produce living creatures; that's one way we can view it.

The second way that Adam, the man, was formed, or as we may put it these days "formatted" was for the specific purpose of God's Son being born of human offspring. Adam needed to be configured accordingly to accommodate the seed that would eventually be born 76 generations later. Eve, Adam's wife, was made from Adam and contained the same DNA. God took time and effort to make sure that the line that led to Christ's birth was kept true to Adam's line. Intermarrying was not allowed (Deut 7:3), along with quite a host of other instructions concerning sexual behavior.

Thirdly, we can view "the LORD God formed man from the dust of the ground" in Genesis 2 as the LORD God forming the "character" of Adam, particularly while Adam is going through his early years. All parents have a part to play in forming the character of their children. The word "form" is not used in Genesis 1 when we read that living creatures were created from the ground. The Hebrew word used for "form" relates to the way a potter forms a piece of pottery. In Jeremiah we read,

The Center of Civilization

> "Can I not do with you, Israel, as this potter does?" declares the LORD. "Like clay in the hand of the potter, so are you in my hand, Israel." (Jer 18:6)

In this verse the Lord is talking about forming the character of the people, he wants to "form" their hearts to be like his own righteous heart. The Hebrew word for "formed" is *yatsar* and is used when speaking of forming the people of Israel's character. That process started with Adam who was their forefather. Yatsar is the root word in Genesis chapter 2 and in Jeremiah chapter 18. So forming someone's character, personality, or spiritual qualities is another way we can view the phrase, "the LORD God formed man from the dust of the ground." God was rearing up a man from the lowly position in which he found himself. Therefore, we realize that time needs to be taken when forming someone's character: children spend years learning from their parents.

The "forming" thread continues if we look at the phrase in Genesis 2: "the LORD God formed man from the dust of the ground." Humanity as we know it—modern humans—had been created back in Genesis 1 and "Adam" was their collective name. However, Adam the man, whom God took to the garden of Eden, was an individual. He represented the "collective Adam"; in other words, he represents us all. The New Testament refers to Adam as one "who is a pattern of the one to come" (Rom 5:14). Adam the man was a pattern, figure, or type who represents human beings and because Christ also became a human being, Adam is a type of Christ too.

The chain of generations that led to Christ's birth started with Adam. God chose a man from among men to start this process. Adam, the man, was born as we all were. We cannot be human unless we are born from a previous generation of human beings—excepting the very first generation into whom God placed his image. Adam the man was born from the mating of two human beings, male and female, but God is going to breathe into him in a special way, and a new era will have begun. We see a distinction between Adam the collective group in Genesis chapter 1 and Adam the individual in Genesis chapter 2. This is highlighted well in Genesis chapter 5 where we see the Hebrew word "adam" used both as a collective noun and a proper noun—the proper noun being "Adam" the man's personal name, and the collective noun being the generic name for mankind. The NIV translates the Genesis passage this way:

> This is the written account of Adam's family line. When God created mankind, he made them in the likeness of God. He created

God and Primordial People

them male and female and blessed them. And he named them "Mankind" when they were created. When Adam had lived 130 years, he had a son in his own likeness, in his own image; and he named him Seth. (Gen 5:1–3)

The Hebrew text in these verses uses the word "adam" four times, yet in English the NIV translators have written "Mankind" twice in place of adam. That is because the first mention is the proper noun and the second and third are the collective noun and the fourth is the proper noun again. Strong's concordance has two different numbers for the two words; there is "adam 120" the collective noun, and "Adam 121" the proper noun. In the Westminster Leningrad Codex the Hebrew marking surrounding the words for adam the proper noun and adam the collective noun, are slightly different: אָדָם and אָדָֽם. The consonants and vowel pointings are the same but the phonetic pronunciation is different.

The text of Genesis itself supplies us with answers about the individual man, Adam, and the collective group Adam. This is how the King James Version translates the Genesis 5 passage:

> This *is* the book of the generations of Adam. In the day that God created man, in the likeness of God made he him; Male and female created he them; and blessed them, and called their name Adam, in the day when they were created. And Adam lived an hundred and thirty years, and begat *a son* in his own likeness, after his image; and called his name Seth. (Gen 5:1–3)

The King James Version only changes one of the "adam" words into "man," the other three are left as "Adam" even though the "collective group "Adam" is meant for the third one, which is why the word "them" is used. So we are not talking about an individual because God made them male and female, and called their name Adam. The translators of the King James Bible are trying to help us understand the allegorical nature of the story so that when we come to chapter 2 of Genesis and the individual man named Adam is introduced to us, we will see that he is representing all the other "adam/humankind."

Regarding the translation of "Adam," it would be wrong of us to decide that one Bible version is correct while the other is wrong because the allegorical nature of Adam being both a collective group and an individual is a part of the objective of Genesis. Even the Leningrad Codex (the oldest complete edition of the Hebrew Bible that we have, dating to around AD 1008 to 1010) cannot be said to be the preferred version, the pointing system they used was their opinion of where the "proper name" for Adam ought to be appropriate and where the "collective noun" ought to fit into the text.

It is apparent to translators that two ways of using the word "Adam" exist because the context of the narrative demands it to be so. For instance, in Genesis chapter 1 "the Adam" were told to "fill the earth" but in Genesis chapter 2 Adam is located in one place (the garden of Eden). Also in Genesis 1 both male and female are named Adam but in Genesis 2 the female is not named Adam she is named Eve. We see that the text is talking about the individual Adam in the garden at this point.

Chapter 15
Train Up a Child

IN GENESIS CHAPTER 1 God called humankind "Adam," both male and female were called Adam. But in Genesis chapter 2 we begin to hear about one particular man who is called Adam and his wife is called Eve, not Adam. The ambiguity of the text is deliberate. Adam, the collective name for the human race runs seamlessly into Adam, the individual who represents the human race.

Given that us human beings are naturally inquisitive we will want to ask: how was Adam the man chosen for this task?

The intentional parallels in the early chapters of Genesis mean we will not get a textbook understanding of neatly arranged points. There is a mystery enshrouding the early chapters of Genesis, but slowly humankind is starting to see the cloak lifted. What lies beneath astounds us with its depth and breadth and also humbles us when we see the initiation of the plan of our salvation. Had we not fallen from the height in which we were made there would be no need for the Bible at all. God's law would still be in our hearts and not on paper or papyrus. God's law of love was committed to papyrus in order that it may be committed within our hearts. Those who hunger and thirst for righteousness will be filled, those who enquire in a nonchalant manner will not receive. But those who seek will find, which means there is some seeking to be done.

> So was fulfilled what was spoken through the prophet: "I will open my mouth in parables, I will utter things hidden since the creation of the world." (Matt 13:35)

There are answers waiting for us if we look. The theme of an abandoned baby crops up in the scriptures and the theme ought to mean something to us because it is mentioned more than once, as if someone is saying, "Have you noticed this?"

> On the day you were born your cord was not cut, nor were you washed with water to make you clean, nor were you rubbed with salt or wrapped in cloths. (Ezek 16:4)

But where did this take place? Verse 3 highlights that "Your origin and your birth are from the land of the Canaanite, your father was an Amorite and your mother a Hittite." If these verses are throwing a little light onto Adam's birth we see that he was a child of mixed parentage, which may not have stood well with the two people groups mentioned, so the parents decided that abandonment was the best option for them. The Amorite and Hittite people may not have been the exact names of the nations to which the parents belonged, since the Hittites were based around Anatolia and the Amorites were roving people. If one of Adam's parents came from the Anatolian region and another from a nomadic tribe, the people Ezekiel was talking to would relate to the story. Even though they may not have known the name for the people who lived in Anatolia in 5000 BC, they would understand that it's the region where the Hittites originate, because some Hittites traveled and lived in Canaan where the Hebrews would learn of their history.

The story Ezekiel relates begins in verse 2 by saying, "Son of man, confront Jerusalem with her detestable practices." God is talking to the "people" of Jerusalem, and at that time Jerusalem was occupied by Jews. The city of Jerusalem itself had a convoluted history going back to 4500 BC. David captured the city from the Jebusites. The Hittites and Amorites don't seem to come into the picture of the city of Jerusalem. And if we are talking about the birth of the Jewish nation per se we have to go back to Abraham and Sarah, neither of whom were Amorite or Hittite. But if we are going back to the genealogical root then we have to go back to Adam. Perhaps the clue is laid before us when the Lord begins his instructions to Ezekiel by calling him "Son of man," which of course in Hebrew is "Son of Adam."

Ezekiel's story is a prophetic allegory not a precise definition of what happened years ago, but we ought to take note that "No one looked on you with pity or had compassion enough to do any of these things for you. Rather, you were thrown out into the open field, for on the day you were born you were despised. Then I passed by and saw you kicking about in your blood, and as you lay there in your blood I said to you, 'Live!' I made you grow like a plant of the field. You grew and developed and entered puberty. Your breasts had formed and your hair had grown, yet you were stark naked" (6–7). The parallels to the story of Adam and Eve abound.

Moses told the new nation of Israel to "Remember the days of old; consider the generations long past" (Deut 32:7). Moses continues by explaining what happened in generations long past. "In a desert land he found him, in a barren and howling waste. He shielded him and cared for him; he guarded him as the apple of his eye, like an eagle that stirs up its nest and hovers over its young, that spreads its wings to catch them and carries them aloft. The Lord alone led him; no foreign god was with him. He made him ride on the heights of the land and fed him with the fruit of the fields. He nourished him with honey from the rock, and with oil from the flinty crag, with curds and milk from herd and flock and with fattened lambs and goats, with choice rams of Bashan and the finest kernels of wheat. You drank the foaming blood of the grape" (10–14). Moses is also using allegorical language but once again the resemblance to Adam's story is strong.

Adoption is a theme that runs through the Bible. For example Romans 8:15 says, "the Spirit you received brought about your adoption to sonship. And by him we cry, 'Abba, Father.'" If we think of Adam as an illustration of "adoption to sonship" we see that Adam did receive a measure of God's Spirit because God breathed into him. He also received adoption into God's family: God was his father and planted fruit trees for his nourishment and provided an area for Adam to live. Adam is an example of what God can do for each one of us. Psalm 27:10 (NASB) says, "For my father and my mother have forsaken me, But the Lord will take me up." We can view this verse prophetically regarding Jesus, the second Adam, and we can also see it as a reference to the first Adam. Abandoning a child is a rare occurrence but it does happen. David wrote the Psalm and he was still living happily at home with his father Jesse as a young man. Jesus asked God, his father, "Why have you forsaken me?" But the mother of Jesus was not far away. The theme of a baby being abandoned by both parents, and the Lord taking care of him, seems to have happened at some point. The Bible uses the scenario for us to learn lessons and also seems to allude to an historical event. Adam fits the criteria for being that baby.

At the outset of Christ's genealogical line we find Adam, the adopted son of God. We ought not to say that Adam was God's firstborn because Jesus was the firstborn Son of God. "When God brings his firstborn into the world, he says, 'Let all God's angels worship him'" (Heb 1:6). God was the father of baby Jesus and Mary was his mother. God created human beings but he had never been a physical father before, humans could call God "Creator" but only Jesus could call him father in the physical sense of the word. Those who are "born of the Sprit" may also call God, father, but that is because we are his spiritual children not his physical children. We all have human fathers, except for Christ who had God as the father of his physical body. The birth of Jesus was the first time God had physically fathered a son, hence Jesus was God's "firstborn." Joseph, Mary's husband, adopted Jesus in the same way that the LORD God adopted Adam back in southern Mesopotamia all those years ago.

Let us suppose for the moment that Adam had been an abandoned baby left in the open field, a deserted barren and howling waste as Ezekiel and Moses imply. The open field and desert land are dusty places, and particularly dusty in those days when much of the land lay uncultivated. We can view the phrase, "the LORD God formed a man from the dust of the ground" (Gen 2:7), actually to mean "dust." Adam was taken from the dust in which he lay as a helpless baby and at some point later arrived in the welcoming garden of Eden.

So let us move forward with Adam being adopted by the LORD God and taken to the sparsely populated area of southern Mesopotamia, where the beginnings of crop cultivation were taking place in the Neolithic Revolution, and where God taught Adam about cultivating fruit trees. In fact "cultivation" is a word that Genesis chapter 2 uses in regard to Adam's work.

> Then the LORD God took the man and put him into the garden of Eden to cultivate it and keep it. (Gen 2:15 NASB)

Scripture has a way of getting to the point, but we would be wise to understand that many years could have taken place between events that are mentioned in the early chapters of Genesis. God breathed into Adam, and we can say that God has breathed into humanity when we were made in his image, and we would be correct. But Adam was breathed into in a way that would start a chain of events leading to the human race eradicating the blemish of which we are blighted.

One change that Genesis wants us to take notice of is the length of years Adam lived. Adam was 130 years old before his son Seth was born. The Septuagint (which has greater accuracy regarding numbers and from which Stephen in the New Testament quotes) states that Adam was 230 years old when Seth was born.

God and Primordial People

Adam, and his offspring up to the tenth generation, seem unable to father children until they were well over 100 years old. We also see that they died between 700 and 1,000 years old, although none of them actually made it to 1,000 years, (unless we include Enoch who had no recorded death and seems to be still alive). Adam (and his family) had each phase of his life elongated—a longer childhood, lengthened adolescence, a protracted middle age, and an extended old age. The average lifespan of Adam and his immediate posterity was lengthened by a factor of 10. For most men it is possible to become a father in their teenage years. Seth was 205 when his first child was born and he lived to be 912. So if we move the decimal point one place to the left, he was, comparatively speaking, 20 years and 6 months old when he became the father of Enosh, and Seth was 91 years 2 months old when he died. These are ages that would be normal in our present-day world.

The book of Genesis is not alone in attributing extended lives to certain individuals. The Sumerian King List shows extremely long lives for its kings, until after the flood when the length of the Sumerian kings' reigns start to fall.

There is also the Greek writer Hesiod, in the eighth century BC, who spoke of the "Ages of Man," in which he enlightens his readers to the history of a race of people who lived long lives. The people who lived these long lives remained children for extended periods and could spend up to a hundred years at their mother's side. But when they finally grew to full stature they could not keep from sinning or doing wrong to one another, and because they would not give honor to the gods they were put away. Hesiod called these people "silver" because before the silver race there was a golden race of human beings. The golden race lived without sorrow of heart, free from grief and toil. "The fruitful earth unforced bare them fruit abundantly and without stint. They dwelt in ease and peace."[1] Neither did they lose vigor in old age; their limbs remained strong. "When they died, it was as though they were overcome with sleep."[2] Hesiod's writing seems to ring true to the writing within Genesis: there were original people, whom we may think of as a golden race, for these early people of planet earth were true, upright in nature, and innocent of great transgression. Adam, who we read about in Genesis 2 could be likened to the father of the silver race, his offspring did indeed live long lives. Adam's offspring could not keep from sinning. In

---

1. Hesiod, *Homeric Hymns*, sections 109, 121.
2. Ibid.

fact we read that "the LORD saw that the wickedness of man (Adam's line) was great on the earth, and that every intent of the thoughts of his heart was only evil continually. The LORD was sorry that He had made man on the earth, and He was grieved in His heart" (6:5–6 NASB, my parenthesis).

We also have the Lagash King List, which seems to have been written as a satirical rejoinder by a slightly peeved writer from Lagash in response to the lack of kings of Lagash being mentioned in the Sumerian King List. The scribe from Lagash appears to ridicule the long-livers by pointing out they were children in diapers for a long time, and not only were they slow to grow up they were also dull-witted.

Stories of long-lived people do seem to be there. Hesiod, for instance, clothed his stories in Greek perspective, but who can say that he hadn't heard the stories of long-living people from his parents who heard it from their parents, etc. The storylines will have twists and turns added to them as they move from one generation to the next but the essence of the story implies that a race of people who once lived long, is a part of human history.

We can also see how people with a regular lifespan may have jeered and taunted the parents of the children who didn't seem to grow up as speedily as their children. "Huh! My child is now ready to contribute his share of hard work in the field, where is your child? Is he still running around with no clothes on playing with his make-believe toys? Are you feeding him correctly? Are you teaching him? Why won't he grow? My child has grown capable and strong. What is wrong with yours?" But of course the last laugh was with the long-livers, it was they who would be still in their (apparent) youth when their former antagonists hit old age. There was a decrease in the length of life for Adam's genetic line after the flood but perhaps we can still see a glimmer of the taunting that occurred when Ishmael mocked the young Isaac, as noted in Genesis 21:9. Isaac was 60 when he became a father and 180 when he died, so his childhood would have been longer than people from regular human families or even mixed family races such as Ishmael whose father was Abraham but whose mother was Egyptian. We know that Abraham was keen for his son Isaac to get married and father children, but Abraham didn't send his servant on a mission to find a wife for Isaac until Isaac was around 39 years old. That reveals that Isaac probably wasn't physically mature enough until he reached the 40-year mark. Therefore his childhood would also have been extended.

Once Adam's offspring had grown into adulthood the drawn-out childhood would be over and full maturity and wisdom would attend the long-living people. Some of these long-living people seem to have been recognized in the literature of the times because they were a wonder of the ancient world.

The writer of Genesis expects us to wonder when we hear of the high ages of the children of Adam. That is one reason why he wrote the ages down, we are meant to be astounded. We know that normally people do not live that long, the long lives of the people set them apart as special, we are to watch these people as there is something in them. They had been touched by God and breathed upon by his Spirit. God was preparing the ground in preparation for his own Son to be born into the human race; he chose Adam and then produced Eve so that the genetic line of this couple would lead to Jesus. God slowed down the lifespan of Adam. The clues are there in the text if we look: we have to wait until Genesis chapter 4 before Adam makes love to Eve. The reason Adam was 230 before Seth was born was because the phases of his life had been elongated. He and Eve didn't have sexual intercourse until they had reached physical maturity. Most of us have seen children running around the beach with not a stitch on, no one takes any notice because it's what children do, and the children themselves feel no shame about it. The reason Adam and Eve in the garden "were both naked" and "were not ashamed" is probably because they were children.

Chapter 16

The Long-Livers

With long life I will satisfy him. (Ps 91:16)

THE SUMERIAN KING LIST shows longer lives for the kings before the deluge than the kings who lived after the flood; the long lives tie in with the book of Genesis well. Although we need to take a close look at the Sumerian King List because we learn that the kings before the flood lived to be something like 28,000 years, or 8 Sars as the Sumerians used to measure their time. Adam and his children lived long lives, 900 years or so, but none of his family made it to 1,000 years old, let alone 28,000 years. Why the discrepancy?

The answer probably lies here: the record passed down to us through Abraham, Moses, and the scribes assigned to the task of preserving the scriptures contains the exact years that Adam and his family lived because Adam was aware of how long he'd been alive, Seth too, and all of Adam's successors who were after him right up to the flood. Yes, they did live to be over 900 years old, and this information was passed along the family line all the way to Abraham and Moses, etc., who wrote down the exact amount of years Adam's family members lived, which is preserved for us in the Bible.

The Sumerians, who had normal lifespans, may have found it hard to know exactly how long Adam's family members were alive. For instance, Adam lived to be 930 years old, that means if the average Sumerian man lived 75 years there would have been 12 generations of Sumerians during Adam's lifetime. Adam may or may not have shared with the local Sumerian people how long he'd been alive. Let's say that Adam only told his son Seth and immediate family members and Seth only told his son Enosh and family members, and so on all the way to Abraham and Moses who recorded the precise information. That means the Sumerians would have to get the information of how long Adam had been alive from their own fathers who got it from their fathers and so on. If that was so, then the exact years Adam had lived, according to the local Sumerians, may not be anywhere near as accurate as the information that was passed through Adam's family itself.

The Sumerians knew Adam and his family lived long, but how long, was not so easy for them to quantify. The method they had of measuring time using Sars plays an important role too. Strictly speaking a Sar is 3,600 years. But Irving Finkel, who is an Assyriologist at the British Museum, explains that although Sar means 3,600 the Mesopotamians could use it to mean any number that is large. For instance, today we use the word "myriad" to mean any number that is massive, although strictly speaking, myriad means 10,000. The Sumerians might say "may the moon god keep you well for a Sar, (3,600 years)," which means may you enjoy good health for a long time. Or we may say, "I looked up at the nighttime sky and saw myriads of stars." Both examples mean many.

So to sum up: the exact record is preserved in Genesis but the Sumerian King List may give us glimpses of how other generations who were living at the same time passed the information on to their children. A Sumerian father may say to his son, "I'm not exactly sure how long the chief of Eridu has been alive but he was alive when my grandfather was, and his grandfather before him." So when it was written down in the Sumerian King List several Sars were assigned to the kings before the flood, to show the enormity rather than the accuracy of their length of life.

The LORD God raised Adam, he shaped him and formed him into an upstanding and loving human being. At some point in his long childhood Yahweh took Adam to the garden that had previously been planted. Help with the tending, irrigating, fertilizing, and pruning of the fruit trees could have previously come from angels, who were present at various points of human history. For instance, Genesis 6:4 relates that "The Nephilim were on the earth in those days." The Nephilim were not the angels, they were offspring of a liaison between angels and women from Adam's line. But we see that at different times in the history of the world beings whom we have little knowledge of could have been on the earth. We make a mistake presuming that life on earth has always been as it is now. We do not know what relationship God had with the Neanderthal man. Perhaps such knowledge is not for us to know. Hesiod spoke of a golden race in earth's primeval history. People of the golden race were followed by a silver race and later a

The Long-Livers

bronze race of people who put the metal bronze to work, making armor for themselves. There was also a race of heroes—a god-like race of men who were considered some sort of heroes and labeled as demi-gods.

They were the heroes of old, men of renown. (Gen 6:4)

The NIV labels the Nephilim "heroes of old." Hesiod may not have had the precision that the Bible has regarding these primeval days of civilization but we have to say Hesiod does seem to relate to the point Moses is making when he put together the early chapters of Genesis. Moses writes "heroes of old" because he is making a point of contact between his readers and his narrative. Moses presumes his readers will be familiar with these "heroes" and "men of renown" because they do, after all, have some "renown." Moses explains to us that these Nephilim are the offspring of sons of God and human women, Hesiod's demi-gods are offspring of gods and mortals. There is a parallel between what Moses writes and what the Greeks write.

Hesiod then goes on to write about an age of iron. He obtained this knowledge from his predecessors and marks out for us the ages of man from a Greek perspective. The Bible also agrees, to a certain extent, but God is not going to give us information that really does not concern us. Perhaps God did have some sort of relationship with the Neanderthal races, but the answer Jesus gave to Peter may also apply to us regarding the Neanderthal and any other creatures of our genus. "When Peter saw him, he asked, 'Lord, what about him?' Jesus answered, "If I want him to remain alive until I return, what is that to you? You must follow me" (John 21:21–22).

With the knowledge we currently have access to, we can't say what relationship God had with our forbearers: Homo erectus, Homo Heidelbergensis, or Homo neanderthalensis (who is our closet extinct human relative, known mostly by their nickname, The Neaderthals).

Hesiod's "golden race" lived without distress and they were free from misery. They lost no vigor in their later years with their mobility unhindered by withered limbs. They lay themselves down to die as if going to sleep. Perhaps we see how life was before we fell from the height wherein we were made. Moses himself gives us a glimpse of how life ought to be when living closely to Yahweh. "Moses was a hundred and twenty years old when he died, yet his eyes were not weak nor his strength gone" (Deut 34:7). He climbed Mount Nebo and died. "As our days so shall our strength be" seems to be the original plan for humanity and we still see glimpses of it. Jacob said, "Most blessed of sons is Asher . . . your strength will equal your days" (33:24–25).

Chapter 17

Producing Fruit

By 5000 BC the people in Mesopotamia had forsaken the original lifestyle that God had intended humanity to live, even though the benefits of our initial way of life appear to outweigh the advantages of the sedentary agriculturalist routine. Hunter-gatherers naturally enjoyed keeping fit; they daily viewed changing and picturesque scenery, they ate a multifaceted nutritious diet—malnutrition or lack of food was not a feature of their lives. In contrast, the agricultural diets were often grass-based barley, wheat, rice, etc. Starchy foods can be helpful but are short on protein and certain vitamins and minerals. The superior balanced nourishment and exercise of our early ancestors meant the people spoken of in Genesis chapter 1 had greater physical prowess than the majority of people in Mesopotamia and those in our present day and age.

Men in the early years spoken of in Genesis 1 became expertly efficient as predators and enjoyed the experience of being in a hunting party. They used their ingenuity to skillfully find and capture game. They traveled far and wide in search of prey, using their swiftness and strength to overcome wild animals.

The premier Homo sapiens had time for leisure in climates that required minimal shelter and clothing and they had little in the way of the chores, errands, duties, and responsibilities of our current culture. Small groups of people lived in far-reaching areas. Infectious diseases were unlikely to affect people too badly because the roving lifestyle meant the people moved on before waste accumulated and posed a threat to human health. Meeting other groups of people in those early days was a time for rejoicing rather than a fear of competition or being attacked. The folks of the agricultural revolution were stuck in one place their whole lives, which is sharply contrasted to the lifestyle of the hunter-gatherers.

Hunter-gatherers appear to have been altruistic. After successfully trapping a hefty beast there would be more meat than two or three families could consume, so sharing extra meat with other families encouraged affability. When a hunter came home empty-handed, there was no reason why other men within the group would not give him food and share their meat or catch of fish; for on another occasion the situation could be reversed. The selfless attitude within a group, and of the group itself with other groups made for a well-balanced life with each member of a group having their own wellbeing free from stress and strife.

Hunter-gatherers were not able to store food or amass wealth, rich friendships made a person wealthy. They didn't have building programs, or schemes to make a name for themselves. Each person within a group owned only what he could carry and with nothing to steal, violence was minimal and warfare seems to be nonexistent. But the revolution of the late Neolithic era meant that men had many schemes and building projects. "They said to each other, 'Come, let's make bricks and bake them thoroughly.' They used brick instead of stone, and tar for mortar. Then they said, 'Come, let us build ourselves a city, with a tower that reaches to the heavens, so that we may make a name for ourselves'" (Gen 11:3–4). Adam's son Cain left the Eden area and promptly started his work building a city.

By the Neolithic era, we begin to see a few of the negative characteristics of our own culture. The "many" ruled by the "few," with powerful men taking advantage of disenfranchised or deprived people. Slavery also became a feature. The earliest mention of human slavery is seen in the Mesopotamian Code of Hammurabi and we can see in those records that slavery is already a recognized practice. Living conditions were often cramped in the cities and infectious contagions were able to increase with ease, another feature that we who live today will be all too familiar with. Furthermore, long hours of work would be required, with people assigned to repetitive, mind-numbing work. God saying, "In the sweat of thy face shalt thou eat bread" (Gen 3:19 KJV) is hardly surprising. Bread made from grass-based wheat or barley required some backbreaking work. Clay sickles from Mesopotamia circa 5000 BC abound. My own local museum has one on display and I often marvel when I look at it thinking, *I wonder if Adam used this particular clay sickle?*

God and Primordial People

The Neolithic era fell into the same time period that the garden of Eden was first planted. The workers tending the fruit trees in the garden would have found an equitable boss in Yahweh. The workers cultivating the fields in the areas surrounding the garden would have come from the local Ubaid population. Yahweh does seem to be present among the people in those days. Cain and Abel were able to approach him with apparent ease. Cain was even dismissive with him when he spoke with Yahweh: "Am I my brother's keeper?" Some people were also dismissive with Jesus when he walked around. Jesus was only on earth for around 33 years, how long his father Yahweh walked around we cannot say but he appears to have done so. The people of that time realized little of who was among them. But God often comes to us in disguise, to test us and determine what is inside our hearts. As we have behaved towards the least of people we have behaved towards God.

Work is required for the successful growing of fruit trees. God took Adam to the garden and started the process of teaching him how to nurture fruit trees. Adam himself would need a varied diet and fruit alone would not suffice. But if we look closely we may be able to establish how Adam was nourished. Firstly, all the trees in the garden were not simply fruit trees, the text tells us that "The LORD God made all kinds of trees grow out of the ground—trees that were pleasing to the eye and good for food" (Gen 2:9), so we can probably include nut trees as well as fruit trees. Nuts are a useful source of fats and protein.

Secondly, Moses said that God "fed him with the fruit of the fields. He nourished him with honey from the rock, and with oil from the flinty crag, with curds and milk from herd and flock and with fattened lambs and goats, with choice rams of Bashan and the finest kernels of wheat. You drank the foaming blood of the grape" (Deut 32:13-14). We see a nice compliment of major food groups in Moses's list and we see that animal protein was among them. When Adam's son Abel grew into manhood his work included keeping and tending the flocks (Gen 4:2). Let us clarify some of the items on the list of Moses.

- Alert readers may be quick to note that "Bashan" isn't in Mesopotamia. However, "The rams of Bashan" means the same breed as the rams or bulls in Bashan, which was located to the east of the Sea of Galilee. The King James Version captures the Hebrew well when it says, "rams, of the breed of Bashan." We know that God took animals to the garden for Adam to name, so bulls of this breed could have found their way to the garden simply because they were taken there by the LORD God.

- Wheat was also one of the grains being grown in southern Mesopotamia, so perhaps there was a reciprocating cooperation between the occupants of the garden of Eden and the local Ubaid population. Fruit was freely given to the local people, who responded with their own offerings of wheat, so Moses could later write that Adam was fed with the "finest kernels of wheat."

- In those days people understood that olive trees ought to be planted in proximity to the sea in order to thrive. Modern techniques have improved on that situation but what hasn't changed is the olive tree's bias towards rocky soil and craggy limestone. Eridu and Eden were not far from the Persian Gulf and "oil from the flinty crag" would not be hard to procure.

The parallel meaning in Adam being taken to the garden of Eden highlights God's requirement of fruit from human beings. We need to cultivate fruit and then deliver our produce to God. We are all workers in the garden.

> The fruit of the Spirit is love, joy, peace, forbearance, kindness, goodness, faithfulness, gentleness and self-control. (Gal 5:22–23)

John the Baptist's stark message to the Pharisees and Sadducees was "Produce fruit" (Matt 3:8). The earth is the Lord's and he is looking for fruit from the workers within it.

Jesus told a parable in Matthew 21:28–32: "What do you think? There was a man who had two sons. He went to the first and said, 'Son, go and work today in the vineyard.' 'I will not,' he answered, but later he changed his mind and went. Then the father went to the other son and said the same thing. He answered, 'I will, sir,' but he did not go. Which of the two did what his father wanted? 'The first,' they answered."

That's the parable, which was told to the religious people, chief priests, and elders a few days before Jesus was to be crucified. The local application is that the first son is the "publicans and sinners" and the other son is the "chief priests and elders." But for a wider application into which we are all included notice that one son came "first." God made humans in Genesis chapter 1. The humans became wayward, but over the years many of them have come to follow God's Son.

God and Primordial People

The other son began with the man Adam, whom we read about in Genesis chapter 2. We can trace Adam's genetic line through to Jacob whose 12 sons became the nation of Israel. At first they said they would follow the Father. Moses specifically asked them if they would indeed follow the Lord. "All the people answered together and said, 'All that the Lord has spoken we will do!' And Moses brought back the words of the people to the Lord" (Exod 19:8). But after some time the Father said to Ezekiel, "Son of man, I am sending you to the Israelites, to a rebellious nation that has rebelled against me; they and their ancestors have been in revolt against me to this very day" (Ezek 2:3). When God's Son, Jesus, came to earth the Pharisees, Sadducees, teachers of the law, and the general population rejected him.

According to the parable, Genesis chapter 1 seems to deal with humans who are the "first son" and Genesis chapter 2 tells us about the beginnings of the "other son." Fruit was required from both sons. Therefore I tell you that the kingdom of God will be taken away from you and given to a people who will produce its fruit (Matt 21:43). The chief priests and the Pharisees heard Jesus's parables, they knew he was talking about them (45).

The importance of fruit production is one lesson we learn from the garden of Eden. Jesus told a parable in Luke 13:6–9 about a man who had a fig tree growing in his grounds but did not find fruit on it. So he said to the gardener, "For three years now I've been coming to look for fruit on this fig tree and haven't found any. Cut it down! Why should it use up the soil?" "Sir," the man replied, "let's leave it alone for one more year, and I'll dig around it and fertilize it. If it bears fruit next year, fine! If not, then cut it down." Our duty then is to produce fruit, and we are helpfully told what type of fruit we are to produce in Galatians 5:22–23: "The fruit of the Spirit is love, joy, peace, patience, kindness, goodness, faithfulness, gentleness and self control."

Chapter 18

Educating Adam

THE LORD GOD TOOK on the responsibility of Adam's education and started to teach him.

> Out of the ground the LORD God formed every beast of the field and every bird of the sky, and brought them to the man to see what he would call them; and whatever the man called a living creature, that was its name. (Gen 2:19)

Adam's lessons in zoology could have taken many days and years to complete, similarly to the education of young people these days, but with the added aspect of Adam being a slow learner because of his extended childhood. Adam showed a talent for understanding an animal's nature and naming it accordingly. A name in the Hebrew language expresses the essence and nature of its owner. For this reason naming the animals was no easy task and would require studying a creature's habits, demeanor, and appearance and then applying a suitable name. A student given an assignment of naming animals would probably need to use a one-animal-at-a-time method, where each animal may have been studied and watched for considerably long periods, which would give Adam the time to know and understand the nature, reproductive behavior, and instincts of any given creature. Adam's education would be higher than current university and college courses, even though we have some fine and knowledgeable lecturers and teachers. Adam was being taught by someone who had a keen interest in the biological life of planet earth because he was, after all, the architect and producer of all such life.

The name of an eagle comes from the Hebrew root meaning "to lacerate" or "one who lacerates." The talons on an eagle are razor-sharp; their beak is also sharp and is used for killing their prey. Adam would have taken time to analyze the behavior of a creature and the researching of a particular animal was a part of his education. We sometimes get the picture that the naming of the animals happened quickly and that Adam came up with names in a quick impromptu off-the-cuff manner, but that would not have been the case. Forethought and ingenuity went into this responsibility. Each animal could have taken weeks or months to study and would be used as a school lesson by his wise teacher.

Adam would have studied another bird of prey—the cormorant, of which the Hebrew word is *shalak*, meaning "plunging" or "darting down." This family of birds are fish-eaters, catching their prey by their excellent diving technique. Once underwater they propel themselves with their feet and wings; some cormorant species have been found to dive as deep as 45 meters.

The names of other animals are categorized by the same method. The biblical word for bat implies "flying in the dark." From a jackal or fox we get the meaning of "burrow." The dog "yelps" and the bear is "slow." Lion conveys a sense of "violence" and the name can also mean "to pierce." The leopard's name gives us "to spot or stain as if by dripping." We even see a sense of humor in the leopard's name. A man painting the black guttering of his roof instructs his dog to sit beneath his ladder. Then a passerby says, "Nice Dalmatian you have there." The painter looks down from his ladder and replies, "That's odd, he was a white mongrel before I started painting."

Adam's education took longer than ours. God slowed the process of Adam's life-stages down for a reason. Human beings had left the simple life and had accelerated into "life in the fast lane," so God slowed life down for Adam. He wouldn't be able to run amok with other young people his age because they had matured, while he was still learning. The local youths may have scoffed at Adam and his posterity, but God was teaching Adam, Seth, Enosh, etc. humility in the face of provocation. Adam and his offspring were still blighted with the stain of sin that we all are but their childhood humility, wonder, and willingness to obey lasted far longer than the surrounding people. The reason Abraham asked Sarah to masquerade as his sister and not as his wife was because his fear compelled him to do so. Abraham lived to be 175 years old, and that is still around double the age of what humans live. Perhaps Abraham had been scoffed at as a youngster because his childhood years would have been longer than most, and this may have engendered his fearful outlook of strangers, and also one reason why he kept himself removed from local populations when he traveled in Canaan.

Educating Adam

An imperative aspect of Adam's "forming" by the LORD God (and our own "forming") would be the fostering of humility deep within his heart. The Bible cannot seem to overstate the magnitude of a human being's need for "humility." Any astute reader of the scriptures will soon see that "being humble" is a lesson of immense importance. The word "humility" is even grafted into the word "human."

> Pride brings a person low, but the lowly in spirit gain honor. (Prov 29:3)

Adam was being trained in Yahweh's ways, similar to how early primordial man had been trained. "Make it your ambition to lead a quiet life," said Paul in 1 Thessalonians 4:11. Adam was learning from the master; he was being formed and shaped.

The forming of the animals by God may also have had the secondary purpose of suitable animals being pets or beasts of burden for Adam. Animals can be trained and made useful for human work and we humans often enjoy the time we spend with animals. The word "formed" also means that God could shape the character and upbringing of Adam, training him in righteousness. And although the animals could not be trained in righteousness they could be trained in usefulness, so they too were "formed."

Adam's education also included studying the trees of the garden of Eden. Date palm trees can grow to over 20 meters and the fruit is located near the tops of the trees. Adam would have to learn how to climb the tree to obtain the fruit. Some date palm trees are still harvested by fit, able-bodied people climbing the trunk without safety harnesses. The technique requires skill and endurance. The knowledge of tending, pruning, and climbing the date palm trees was skilled work and would need to be taught to Adam by someone who had the appropriate knowledge. Yahweh himself may have passed on the knowledge, or perhaps local people, or even angels who seem to have been in and around the southern Mesopotamian area at that time. If we go with Yahweh as the teacher then we begin to see the intimate relationship that developed between Yahweh and Adam. God does, after all, want that intimate relationship with each one of us, not only Adam. But our indwelling spot, stain, and sin have put distance between him and us. The hope of the scriptures is that one day God's dwelling will once again be among the people, and "he will dwell with them. They will be his people, and God himself will be with them and be their God" (Rev 21:3).

Chapter 19
Made in the Image of God

WE SEE CHRIST IN the phrase "Let us make man in our image" (Gen 1:26). Not only as the second person of the Trinity issuing the next phase of creation but also as a member of humanity, for "the Word became flesh and dwelt among us" (John 1:14). Christ was "the image of the invisible God" (Col 1:15).

"Let us make man in our image" has a wider application than God merely creating Homo sapiens; something profound was taking place with an ultimate goal far higher than the creation of physical creatures in a physical universe. In 1 Corinthians 15:49 Paul says, "Just as we have borne the image of the earthly man, so shall we bear the image of the heavenly man." Christ came down to earth from heaven and took on our fleshly frame in order that we may be raised to heaven and bear his likeness.

The directive "Let us make man in our image" was a larger operation than we may first perceive. Let us imagine a lump of clay in the hands of a potter. This one lump of clay represents humans, from early primordial man to humans who are alive now and also those who will live in the future. Our collective name was Adam. God is the potter working to shape the clay into a useful vessel but the potter finds that this particular clay has some resistance to it, i.e., our fallen nature and willfulness. So as Genesis chapter 2 gets underway we see the potter take a little piece of that lump of adamic clay (Adam the man) and treat it in a way that will eventually eradicate the resistant flaw in the whole lump of clay. (Similar to the potter we read about in Jeremiah chapter 18.) Let us suppose that the collective Adam, created in Genesis chapter 1, is being shaped into a cup but the cup becomes weak and a hole appears, rendering the container useless. Adam, the man in Genesis chapter 2, is another piece of the same clay; this smaller piece of the original lump of clay is being shaped into a handle, allowing the hole to be plugged and also the vessel to be strengthened, enabling the cup to be lifted higher—for it is helpful if cups have a handle to be lifted in someone's hand. We are, so to speak, "jars of clay," and Christ, helped by his genetic predecessors, is the handle that will lift us higher. We see God taking a tiny piece of the main lump of clay when Adam the man was put into the garden. God started a sequence of events with Adam, the man, that would lead to Christ, God's Son, coming to earth and lifting the human race.

Isaiah 43:21 (KJV) saying, "This people have I formed for myself" may reveal another way of looking at God forming a genetic line for himself. The Spirit of God speaking through Isaiah explains that "this people" or genetic line were formed for God to be physically manifest in the flesh, for "God was in Christ" (2 Cor 5:19 KJV) and Christ was born at the end of the line that Luke lays out neatly for us in the third chapter of his gospel. So in that sense God did form "this people" for himself.

We may ask: why did Christ need any genetic predecessors at all? Why couldn't Christ have come without any predecessors and be born of any woman who was willing? We see a part of the answer to that question in John the Baptist's life. He was sent to "prepare the way for the LORD" (Isa 40:3; also referenced in Matt 3:3). There was some ground to prepare and John played his part. But it was not only John who prepared the way, Moses and the law and the prophets also played their parts in helping to prepare the way. Human beings need to know that we have fallen from the height in which we were created. Our education in these matters started in the early chapters of Genesis. God graciously reveals to us our need, and informs us of our previous history on the planet, along with some information on the formation of the universe itself.

For probably 193,000 years humans lived on the earth without cities, civilization, or the written word. For the early part of those years we lived in an upright manner, treating others as we would like to be treated ourselves. That was the rule, and no paper, papyrus, or scroll was needed to write the rule down because it was written on everyone's heart. People knew, and were aware of the rule. Along the way an enemy corrupted the heart of man and God reluctantly gave us over to that corruption, we were, after all, creatures with freewill. The garden of Eden depicts our state perfectly: God made Homo sapiens with righteousness in our hearts, but we took advice from an adversary and then grasped the control of our own reins turning them rebelliously in a direction that God never intended us to follow. Eve ate the fruit because she desired it to make her wise but consequently she found her childhood innocence had vanished. Humanity also lost its way by taking control of its own "forming," and once disobedience and selfishness became components within us God lifted his hands and started to work on our "forming" another way. God has not given up on us. "For those God foreknew he also predestined to be conformed to the image of his Son" (Rom 8:29). God is still forming us and will "by the power that enables him to bring everything under his control, . . . transform our lowly bodies so that they will be like his glorious body" (Phil 3:21).

We sometimes see in the Psalms and other books of the Bible a distinction between Adam the collective group and Adam the single human being along with his offspring. Scripture does make reference to the bulk of humanity on one hand, and Adam's posterity that includes the human line that led to Christ's birth, on the other.

The line to Christ is of importance when we look at humanity as a whole. The line was taken out of humanity, and worked on by God in a distinct way. The written law was administered through it, psalms and prophecies also came through it, which helped alert us to our plight. The line to Christ and surrounding family members all played their part in lifting humanity. A piece of leavened dough can be added to a larger piece of unleavened dough and consequently leaven the whole lump. Luke knew of the import of the line and highlights it (from Adam to Christ) in his gospel. Earlier Christians also knew of its importance. For instance, Canterbury Cathedral in England has an ancient stained glass window dating from the 1170s representing the people in the genealogy of Christ, from Adam (depicted digging with a spade) to Mary's husband Joseph.

The line is distinct from the rest of humanity. In Psalm 8:4 we read, "what is mankind that you are mindful of them, human beings that you care for them?" The Hebrew word for "mankind" is *enosh* and the word for "human beings" is *adam*. In Isaiah 2:9 (NASB) we read, "the common man has been humbled and the man of importance." In Hebrew the common man is *adam* and the man of importance is *ish*. In Psalm 80:17 we read, "Let your hand rest on the man at your right hand, the son of man you have raised up for yourself." Again we see ish as the man at God's right hand and son of man as the "son of adam." In other words we see Jesus Christ as the line from "Adam in the garden," and humanity in general as the Hebrew word enosh or ish, which includes women or wives as *ishshah*. Adam in the garden devised the name ishshah, which the NASB translates as "woman," or more often as "wife." But before Adam came up with the name ishshah the woman was referred to as *neqebah*, Adam, as we know, had a talent for inventing names, and ishshah fits Eve perfectly, but neqebah translates as "female" and comes from humanity made in Genesis chapter 1, which Adam in the garden recognized as ish. Adam called himself ish when he said, "she shall be called 'woman,' for she was taken out of man" (Gen 2:23), taken out of ish.

Adam in the garden was ish himself, the distinction drawn in scripture is that Adam's progeny led to Christ. Attempts have been made in the past to try and see one race as superior over another and, of course, that is patently untrue. We are all the same lump of clay; we were all made from the "land."

Adam's early offspring had the handicap of an elongated childhood while all other children around them were growing at a normal pace, but Adam's offspring also had the benefit of enduring years. In the Septuagint, Deuteronomy 32:8–9, we are informed that God divided the sons of Adam according to the number of angels, but the Lord himself watched over Jacob's people. This allows us to see that angels helped in the early days of human civilization: they had a particular commission to watch over Adam's offspring, but it was the Lord himself who kept his eye on the seed that was contained within the family of Jacob that would eventually culminate in Christ's birth.

Some of the angels did not rise to their task and instead married some of the daughters of Adam. The daughters of Adam's offspring would live long, so an angel wishing to make his home on earth would have a mate for 900 or so years—a better prospect than a wife who would live for only 70 or 80 years. Plus the females of Adam's posterity had the added attraction that they were fair. "The sons of God saw that the daughters of humans (adam) were beautiful" (Gen 6:2 NASB). And the result of the angels forsaking their commission to look after the branches of Adam's line meant many of Adam's extended family members followed in the footsteps of their father Cain, and went badly astray.

> Then the LORD saw that the wickedness of man (Adam's line) was great on the earth, and that every intent of the thoughts of his heart was only evil continually. (Gen 6:5 NASB)

The flood was sent to restore order, which in the main it did, although there was still some work to do in eradicating the disturbance to the human genome by the angels' DNA entering the gene pool.

God and Primordial People

This kind of trouble was facilitated when God made Eve, which Satan saw as an opportunity to disrupt God's plans to save the human race. Eve's creation was a turning point. Heralding a rare lamentation from Yahweh, "The LORD was sorry that He had made man (Adam singular) on the earth, and He was grieved in His heart" (Gen 6:6 NASB; my parenthesis).

The children's book *The Lion the Witch and the Wardrobe*—the well known Christian allegorical book from The Chronicles of Narnia—refers to the White Witch descending from Lilith, rather than from Eve. Lilith was regarded to be Adam's first wife. Isaiah mentions Lilith, and the Jewish Talmud goes into a little more explanation of how she ought to be regarded. Legend has also played a part, explaining that Lilith was made from earth like Adam, not from Adam's rib like Eve. The man Adam didn't have a first wife of course, but if "man in general" has a history before the man Adam then it's easier to see how these stories came to be. In "The Alphabet of Ben Sira," a medieval Hebrew story, Lilith is named as Adam's first wife, being made from the ground just like Adam. Lilith informs Adam that she and he are equal as a consequence of their identical origins. Adam wasn't pleased with Lilith's attitude and they found themselves at variance with each other. Lilith decided to pronounce the Ineffable Name and then flew away into the air. Isaiah 34:14 (DBT) states "the lilith also shall settle there, and find for herself a place of rest." Various versions of the Bible and Bible commentaries have differing ways of translating "Lilith." A couple of versions translate Lilith as it is in Hebrew, *Lilith*, while others go for "night monster" or "screech owl" or "she demon." There is no doubt that translators and commentaries struggle to find the correct meaning for Lilith. Ellicott's commentary remarks on the King James Version's translation of Lilith as "screech owl," thus "while the 'screech-owl' is the Lilith, the she-vampire, who appears in the legends of the Talmud as having been Adam's first wife."[1]

The ancient name Lilith derives from a Sumerian word for female demons or wind spirits—the lilītu. The lilītu dwell in desert lands. Just how far back these stories of Lilith go is for us to conjecture. If we go back to the stories of Hesiod, people of the "golden race" were earth's first humans, they lived a simple and tranquil life. When they died they became pure spirits who roamed the earth guarding men. We can see a similarity with the pure spirits who roamed the earth and Lilith who also became a spirit, although Lilith in the myths became a spirit of malcontent. Hesiod's stories are of course myths and have to be treated as such, but we also have to

---

1. *Ellicott Bible Commentary*, s.v. "Lilith."

admit that God has not told us everything we might like to know about past generations. What happened to the Neanderthals? Did God relate to them as beings with a soul and spirit? Did they become some sort of spiritual creatures when they died? We don't know! Paul was "caught up to paradise and heard inexpressible things, things that no one is permitted to tell" (2 Cor 12:4). When John had his revelation he said, "I was about to write; but I heard a voice from heaven say, 'Seal up what the seven thunders have said and do not write it down'" (Rev 10:4).

If we take a quick look at Mesopotamia's present human population, we see that there is one people group whose faith seems to go back to ancient Mesopotamian religion. The Yezidi people in northern Iraq believe that they are descended directly from Adam alone, while others come from the lineage of both Adam and Eve. According to the Yezidis, the garden of Eden era corresponds to a Golden Age of wisdom and prosperity that once covered the planet. But humankind started to become self-serving and darkness set in. Floods were then released to cleanse the earth. We again see shadows of biblical teaching.

Chapter 20
Forefathers

You were not redeemed with perishable things like silver or gold from your futile way of life inherited from your forefathers. (1 Pet 1:18)

THE HEBREW WORD TOLEDOTH means "genealogy" or "family line." Toledoths are an important feature of the book of Genesis, and the first of the eleven toledoths begins by saying, "This is the account of the heavens and the earth when they were created" (2:4). Adam the man appears to have had the phases of his life stretched out, and it was he who began the process of Christ's descent from heaven to earth. God altered Adam's rate of growth by breathing into his being. As a result, Adam's genetic structure was recoded; he was transformed into a human vessel that would live long, exude health and fitness, be robust, and able to produce seed that would generate the human body of Jesus over 70 generations later.

Eve did not have a human father or mother; she emerged from Adam who did have human parents. Adam's frame carried the blemish that all humans have since we adopted sin. We notice that Adam was quick to eat the fruit of the tree of the knowledge of good and evil and displayed no resistance; he did not remonstrate with his wife, but followed like a sheep to the slaughter. Eve carried the sinful spot because Adam carried it, and so did all their offspring, along with the rest of humanity, that is why Paul relates in Romans chapter 1 that we have been "given over" to it. Furthermore in a similar way, Lucifer the angel gave himself over to pride, jealousy, and anger. Creatures with freewill need to guard their hearts. The Bible warns us to "Watch over your heart with all diligence, For from it flow the springs of life" (Prov 4:23 NASB). Satan has become what he is: resolutely evil with no return to his former innocence. Human beings live in time and space, and hence, redemption is a possibility for us.

Since the fall of humankind Jesus was the sole man, born of a woman, without the "spot." He is without spot or blemish. Faith in Christ saves us from the law of sin and death, and the "futile way of life inherited from your forefathers" (1 Pet 1:18). Jesus had a human mother but not a human father, so he shared in our humanity but he did not inherit the flaw or blemish the rest of humanity has. The human "heart is deceitful above all things and beyond cure" (Jer 17:9). Jesus did not have that deceitful heart but he did have the human frame that we all share. Our humanity is attached to the deceitful heart, therefore we cannot save ourselves. Our human frame is destroyed easily enough when we die but so too is our heart because its deceitful nature cannot survive in God's good kingdom. That's why we are told to "fear Him who is able to destroy both body and soul" (Matt 10:28 NASB). If we are to be rescued from the stain that soils us someone is required to destroy the human frame, someone who does not possess the deceitful heart. We have the human frame and the deceitful heart but Christ had the human frame but not the deceitful heart. Christ alone could rescue humanity from the mess we have carved out for ourselves, and he alone could destroy the grip of sin that holds humanity.

The impure spirits (demons) were able to see that Christ was the one man who did not have the spot or blemish that presently blights the rest of humankind: "In the synagogue there was a man possessed by a demon, an impure spirit. He cried out at the top of his voice, 'Go away! What do you want with us, Jesus of Nazareth? Have you come to destroy us? I know who you are—the Holy One of God!'" (Luke 4:33-24). The impure spirit may not have been privy to God's plan of salvation but he could see, being spiritual in nature, that here was a man who did not have the spiritual spot that stains the souls of all other human beings.

Jesus was crushed, bruised, and killed because of the flaw. Humanity needed to be thrown out and discarded and Jesus did that on our behalf and was able to do it because he shared in our humanity. The human frame that had been "given over" to the spot and corruption was flogged by the Roman soldiers, mocked and punched by the teachers of the law and elders. "Then they spit in his face and struck him with their fists. Others slapped him and said, 'Prophesy to us, Messiah. Who hit you?'" (Matt 26:67–68). Christ's human frame was then nailed to a cross until it expired. Thus the "spot" in humanity had been dealt with and destroyed.

God and Primordial People

While this anger and venom (inspired by the serpent himself) was proceeding from those accusing Jesus, they little realized that Christ was disarming the deadly device that held humanity in its power. Christ "disarmed the powers and authorities, he made a public spectacle of them, triumphing over them by the cross" (Col 2:15). Satan's work was undone in a moment. The spiritual malaise that attaches itself to humankind could now be lifted, demolished, and destroyed. Christ did not have the deceitful corrupted heart that we possess so he was not held down by mortality and instead rose above death, his spirit having rule over his body, unlike our bodies that rule over our spirits. Had not Christ said, "Destroy this temple, and I will raise it again in three days" (John 2:19)? John goes on to explain, "But the temple he had spoken of was his body" (21). Christ had also said, "I lay it down of my own accord. I have authority to lay it down and authority to take it up again" (10:18).

Faith in Christ rescues us from the law of sin and death. Faith is a spiritual attribute, therefore once faith is in place in our spiritual heart Christ's goodness floods into our being and our deceitful heart is blotted out.

> Have mercy on me, O God, according to your unfailing love; according to your great compassion blot out my transgressions. Wash away all my iniquity and cleanse me from my sin.... Surely I was sinful at birth, sinful from the time my mother conceived me.... Create in me a pure heart, O God, and renew a steadfast spirit within me. (Ps 51:1–2, 5, 10)

The route taken into the human heart is through the spirit. Spiritual forces are unseen but according to scripture, are far more important than physical forces. Once we are "in Christ" through faith, Colossians 2:20 informs us that we "died with Christ to the elemental spiritual forces of this world." In Christ's death we all died: it only took one human being to die the perfect death and because humans are all linked physically we can all avail ourselves of the benefits of Christ's "death and resurrection" by faith, which is our route into Christ and his route into us. He stands at the door of our hearts and knocks (Rev 3:20).

"Let us make man in our image, after our likeness" reads Genesis 1:26 (KJV), therefore man has the image and likeness of God, which means some of the attributes associated with God must be ours too. One of the first attributes we notice that God has is his ability to create. We also have that ability to create. But I am not here talking about our creative flair for art, fashion, or architecture. I am talking about our ability to actually place something into creation that wasn't there before. In fact I ought to say some*one* rather than some*thing*. A human male and female are able to bring a new human being into creation. We sometimes talk of responsible family planning, and it appears that God has given that responsibility to human beings. It is we who decide when, where, and how many new people are brought into being. We are endued with an awesome ability. God has allowed us to add our own creative acts into the universe.

> God blessed them and said to them, "Be fruitful and increase in number." (Gen 1:28)

When a human being is born the child receives the physical attributes of his parents—50 percent of the DNA from each parent—but the infant also receives the "futile way of life" from its father (according to the scripture, "inherited from your forefathers" [1 Pet 1:18]). God endued the first human beings with the ability to pass on to their offspring not only their genes, (something that all biological life is able to do) but also their spiritual state too. (Something that animal life is not able to do.) So our first parents began the process of propagating planet earth with their offspring, passing on genes and the human spirit. At some point the human spirit became polluted by way of human beings seeking their own ungodly ways inspired by the deceptive spirit we know as Satan. So God "gave them over" or "allowed it to happen." From that point on, God, wishing to overcome the darkness that had entered into the human psyche, looked for an opportunity to begin his work of redemption. He chose a man and called him Adam, after "man" in general. God then altered this particular man's growth by breathing into his frame, slowing the stages of his development down quite dramatically.

Moses, who is credited with writing Genesis, recorded that Adam lived to be 930 years old expecting his readers to be astounded. Moses's writings require us to use our own initiative and fill the gaps he leaves in the text of Genesis. Moses was not neglectful—leaving holes for us to fill in arbitrarily—he supposes that creatures with "wit and understanding" will use their attributes and apply "context" where it is needed. When someone asked me, "How did Eve know that she ought not to eat from the tree of the knowledge of good and evil?" I understood why they asked—Eve wasn't created when God told Adam not to eat from the tree. Moses, expecting us to use "context" when we read his writings, gives us the answer once we put that context into play. When families get together, they talk, they tell each other anything important they think their family members ought to know.

God and Primordial People

So the answer to their question is: Adam told Eve about the restriction of eating the fruit from the tree of the knowledge of good and evil. That's why the serpent came to Eve and said, "Did God really say, 'You must not eat from any tree in the garden'?"

So when we read about the age of the patriarchs when they fathered children, or the great age they lived until they died, we are supposed to be startled. Moses considered the ages of Adam's family members important enough to disclose. Moses expects us to place the context around the information he gives us, so if Seth was 205 when he became the father of Enosh and 912 when he died, we are expected to join the dots. The phases of Seth's life, along with the other patriarchs, had been stretched out to a speed 10 times slower than ours. In normal lifespan terms Seth was 20 years and 6 months old when he fathered his first child and was a little over 91 years old when he died.

The curtailment of growth within Adam's direct offspring also seems to have affected their ability to learn. The aim of this slowness to learn could be to engender humility within the Adamic clan, although it didn't always work, as we see with Cain. When the words "Adam" and "ish" are mentioned closely together in the Old Testament, it is Adam who is considered of "low estate." When we read in Psalm 62:9, "Surely the lowborn are but a breath, the highborn are but a lie," it is Adam who is considered lowborn and ish is considered the highborn. The elongation of the phases of life for Adam's family started to drop severely after the flood.

> Then the LORD said, "My Spirit shall not strive with man forever, because he also is flesh; nevertheless his days shall be one hundred and twenty years." (Gen 6:3 NASB)

God needed to remind Adam's offspring that they too were flesh, just like the surrounding people: the Ubaid, Sumerian, and Akkadian populations who lived regular lifespans.

Noah seems to have married a woman with a regular lifespan or mixed lifespan parentage, because from Noah's children onwards the lifespans decreased. Sarah still contained some of the life-phase elongation, which is why we see her good looks maintained in her older years; though she was over 60 she could still attract the attention of both Pharaoh and Abimilech. But by the time we get to King David the lifespan is 70 years.

God had originally given the control for population growth to human beings, but now that humanity had "gone wrong" God needed to step in. Adam in the garden of Eden spent many years slowly learning God's will, being taught by the ever patient Yahweh. Adam was joined by Eve at some point early on in life. Normally, human females are born as a product of their fallen parents, but Yahweh begins steps to break the chain of cause and effect. Eve did not enter the world the same route as other females.

The writer to the Hebrews says, "Therefore, when Christ came into the world, he said: 'Sacrifice and offering you did not desire, but a body you prepared for me'" (Heb 10:5). The writer is quoting the Septuagint translation of Psalm 40:6, and the preparation of Christ's body started with Adam and Eve in the garden. God produced a woman from Adam's stem cells. God was beginning his own human family. This was not the will of a husband or any human agent but God was at work preparing for the entrance of his Son into the world. We do not read of Adam being consulted about the creation of Eve, this was God's family and hence, Christ's family. That's why John tells us, "He came to that which was his own, but his own did not receive him" (John 1:11). Christ came to those who were his own family, they were his family before he was even born, but they rejected him. But John continues, "Yet to all who did receive him, to those who believed in his name, he gave the right to become children of God—children born not of natural descent, nor of human decision or a husband's will, but born of God" (12–13).

Paul, in 2 Corinthians 5:17, enlightens us to the fact that anyone who is in Christ is a new creation. Paul also educates us to the fact that

> We were therefore buried with him through baptism into death in order that, just as Christ was raised from the dead through the glory of the Father, we too may live a new life. (Rom 6:4)

Isaiah begins his prophecies by calling on heaven and earth:

> Hear me, you heavens! Listen, earth! For the LORD has spoken:
> "I reared children and brought them up, but they have rebelled against me." (Isa 1:2)

The first toledoth written in Genesis is that of the "heavens and the earth." The second toledoth is Adam's. So the first generating of heaven joining with earth belongs to no human agency but to God. God's plan to bring his Son from heaven to earth is the first toledoth.

Adam represented man and was taken from man. Men, as we have read, have a fallen nature that God has given them over to, men then pass on their fallen nature to the next generation. Peter remarks about the "futile way of life inherited from your forefathers" (1 Pet 1:18). Moses told us that

God and Primordial People

"in the iniquities of their fathers shall they pine away" (Lev 26:39). Fathers are singled out as the carrier of the fallen nature. Women certainly have a fallen nature too but the men seem to be the carriers. The Bible uses the phrase "sins of the fathers," and alludes to similar phrases but we don't read of the "sins of the mothers," it is fathers who are singled out for us to watch.

> I, the LORD your God, am a jealous God, visiting the iniquity of the fathers on the children. (Exod 20:5 NASB)

We can easily miss the importance of the phrase "sins of the fathers" thinking that a deed the fathers have committed affects their posterity in a circumstantial way. For instance, if a man decides to steal something and gets caught, his family will have to fend for themselves while the man of the house is paying his debt to society in prison. So in that way the sin of the father (theft) directly affects his children who now have no father figure in their life. Furthermore, regarding iniquity of the fathers we are not talking about "generational curses," which was a popular point of view in some quarters of the church a few years ago. The phrase "sins of the fathers" highlights the fallen nature being passed from one generation to the next through the fathers. Let us remember that it was the men who needed to be circumcised, no such ruling existed for women. The act of circumcision directly affects the organ of the physical body used for procreation. God uses many ways of speaking to us and drama, parallels, shadows, poems, types, the natural world, and physical alterations of the human body all count towards the big picture God is painting.

We may think that the sinful contamination is only functional for three or four generations, as the Lord explained in Exodus 20:5, "I, the LORD your God, am a jealous God, visiting the iniquity of the fathers on the children, on the third and the fourth generations of those who hate Me," but if each generation in turn has no resistance to the malign spiritual contagion then they in turn pass the fallen state on to another four generations, who will subsequently pass it on to their progeny. We read in Romans that God "gave them over" and we see another aspect when God says he will "visit the iniquity" on the children. The unwieldy nature of shaping human beings who possess freewill means God will only strive with us for so long.

> My spirit shall not always strive with man. (Gen 6:3 KJV)

We are here talking about original sin being passed further into humanity and not punishment for specific wrongdoing because Ezekiel explains that "The child will not share the guilt of the parent, nor will the parent share the guilt of the child. The righteousness of the righteous will be credited to them, and the wickedness of the wicked will be charged against them" (Ezek 18:20), or as Jeremiah puts it, "whoever eats sour grapes—their own teeth will be set on edge" (Jer 31:30). So in the iniquity being visited onto the children we see original sin and not punishment for specific sin.

The King James Version labels a specific malady that humankind is afflicted with as "concupiscence."

> But sin, taking occasion by the commandment, wrought in me all manner of concupiscence. (Rom 7:8)

Concupiscence, in this verse, pertains to our lower appetites and manifests itself contrary to reasoning. Normally our biological desires serve a useful function, such as a desire to eat, or our desire to have sex, or desire to exercise or rest, etc. These are common biological appetites that we ought to listen to and obey when they occur in the ordinary way that God intended them to be used—at the right time, in the right place, and for the right duration.

There seems to be three ways concupiscence manifests itself. Firstly, concupiscence can take an ordinary good biological desire and urge us to indulge the desire inappropriately, perhaps at the wrong time or for the wrong length of time or wrong place. For instance, resting is good and something we all need to do, but if we rest all the time we can no longer call our behavior "rest" because the vice of laziness has taken over. As Ecclesiastes 3:1 tells us, "There is a time for everything and a season for every activity." Yet concupiscence overrides the appropriate amount of time for a given activity and overbalances a person in such a way that we are similar to children's clown toys that have a spherical lower body in place of legs causing them to roll from one side to the other. Hosea explained that the people of Ephraim were "hot as an oven" and like "a flat loaf not turned over" (Hos 7:7–8). Some cooking requires the food to be turned at the halfway point, and failing to do so will mean the food is burned on one side and undercooked on the other. Similarly concupiscence creates a disproportionate balance resulting in an inability for us to stand upright, we begin to sway and slump when we ought to be straight, steady, and strong. Hosea continued, saying, "Ephraim is like a dove, easily deceived and senseless—now calling to Egypt, now turning to Assyria" (7:11), Egypt in the south, Assyria to the north—like a pendulum we swing from one extreme to the other.

The second way concupiscence operates is in actions that are not ordinary; the King James Bible translators call these actions "inordinate." Paul highlighted that humans were "given over" to the "degrading of their bodies with one another" (Rom 1:24). The degrading of the body serves little or no useful biological function—this is the second way that concupiscence works. For instance, sadomasochism is an appetite that some people have and its place does not seem to fit in the biologically created order. Sadomasochism is one of several appetites that human beings may have, but in this particular appetite one person may enjoy being hurt, and normally our bodies do all they can to avoid being hurt. Our five senses help us to protect ourselves from harm. But if our mind lowers these defenses, or degrades them as we may downgrade someone's salary or their position of rank, then we get closer to what the Bible means when speaking of the "degrading of their bodies." Whipping or torturing a human being is a downgrading of how human beings ought to be treated whether it is for the extraction of information from a suspect or because someone enjoys inflicting pain on another human being. Yet because of an "appetite" some people seem happy to hurt, or to be hurt, in this way. The appetites that serve no useful biological purpose are not acquired; we are, according to scripture, born with them as a part of the package of our fallen nature. However, if we feed them they will get stronger. "Make no provision for gratifying your earthly cravings" (Rom 13:14 WNT).

The third way concupiscence infiltrates the human condition is by lowering our mind's resistance to the sinful desires we find inside us.

We can conclude that the three ways Paul informs us that we have been "given over" work together: number one, not only do we use poor time and place judgement for ordinary desires, but number two, we also have inordinate appetites, and number three our resistance to them is lowered. Paul highlighted firstly, the "degrading of their bodies with one another" (Rom 1:24), secondly, that "God gave them over to shameful lusts" (26), and thirdly, "God gave them over to a depraved mind, so that they do what ought not to be done" (28). The Apostle John highlights three faults in humanity this way: "Everything in the world—the lust of the flesh, the lust of the eyes, and the pride of life—comes not from the Father but from the world" (1 John 2:16).

There are of course other sinful vices that lead us deeper into the mire. "The acts of the flesh are obvious: sexual immorality, impurity and debauchery; idolatry and witchcraft; hatred, discord, jealousy, fits of rage, selfish ambition, dissensions, factions and envy; drunkenness, orgies, and the like. I warn you, as I did before, that those who live like this will not inherit the kingdom of God" (Gal 5:19–21).

This is the "spot" spoken of by Moses. The blemish we all have. James reminds us that "Pure religion" requires a man "to keep himself unspotted from the world" (Jas 1:27 KJV).

Yahweh gave Adam in the garden the best opportunity possible to live with "pure religion." But he was blighted along with the rest of us.

Chapter 21
Appointed to Die

> Precious in the sight of the LORD is the death of his faithful servants.
> (Ps 116:15)

WE SOMETIMES HEAR THAT sin and death only entered the world when Adam fell in the garden of Eden. I highlighted Romans chapter 5 in *Genesis for Ordinary People*, which speaks of sin being in the world before the law that Adam was given, but there is also 1 Corinthians 15:21–22 to consider: "For since by a man came death, by a man also came the resurrection of the dead. For as in Adam all die, so also in Christ all will be made alive." So we'll take a brief look at that verse here.

We need to keep in mind that according to Romans 5:14 Adam is a symbol, a representation or pattern—the NIV reads "a pattern of the one to come." So it's good to remember that what happened in the garden of Eden appears to be a microcosm or model of what was happening in the wider world. Adam in the garden fell, highlighting the fact that the collective Adam mentioned in Genesis chapter 1 also fell. God used the scenario in the garden to show us that we all fall short of the mark he sets. Adam represents Christ because Christ became a man. Adam also represents humanity, hence "Adam" can be singular or plural, i.e., Adam the man or the generic name of the human race. So we can interpret 1 Corinthians 15:21–22 as the King James Version does by saying, "For since by man came death," where "man" means all humans. We can view it as one man too, Adam in the garden who disobeyed, but also as all men everywhere at every stage of human history since God first gave us over to our misdeeds, because we all miss the mark.

Appointed to Die

The word used in Greek for "man" in 1 Corinthians 15:21 is *anthropou*; in Galatians 3:15 the same word is translated as "human"—"Just as no one can set aside or add to a human covenant"—explaining how the word "man" can be used to mean a man or man in general. Let us remember that Ecclesiastes 7:29 says, "Behold, I have found only this, that God made men upright, but they have sought out many devices." The first humans endowed with God's image were upright but they went in search of many schemes. Adam, the man, tells our story.

Death has been a natural factor in biological life since life began. Life and death are used in scripture to highlight "death" as God sees it. Death is not the mere cessation of biological cells ceasing to replicate, death is being cut off from the living God, who is the effervescent fountain of life at the center of reality. Our sins cause that separation. This is one of the momentous and compelling lessons the Bible teaches us—death is separation from God. The Bible will speak of a good man's death as "sleep." There are many who have fallen asleep in Christ and no longer walk the earth, but there are many who are "dead in trespasses and sins" (Eph 2:1) and walk the earth still.

People sometimes ask, "If Adam wasn't the first person to live and die, did God create men sinful because men only die because they sin? And if there were men before Adam in the garden were they sinful, because they died?" The answer is easy for us to see: in the drama displayed for us in the garden of Eden Adam was told he would die on the day he ate from the tree of the knowledge of good and evil, but he didn't die on that day, humanity's spiritual death was the point that God was making. God didn't create us as sinful beings, but he did create us with freewill. And freewill is exactly what it says: free to do wrong as well as right.

The prophet Hosea told the northern people of Ephraim and the southern people of Judea that "like Adam they have transgressed the covenant" (Hos 6:7 NASB), which informs us that Adam had made a covenant with Yahweh. Adam's long years of growing up and slow development helped to maintain his childhood innocence many years longer than regular children. During the span of time that the youthful Adam was without guile, he agreed to abide by the command of the Lord God not to eat fruit from the tree of the knowledge of good and evil. That was the covenant, or contract, between Yahweh and Adam. "Out of the ground the Lord God caused to grow every tree that is pleasing to the sight and good for food" (Gen 2:9), that was Yahweh's side of the contract. There were many trees good for eating and Adam would be abundantly supplied with physical food. In the dramatic scene played out in the garden of Eden we see that one of the trees was called the "tree of life," we see some symbolism that the tree was good for spiritual food. But Adam broke the agreement and lost his place in the garden. Ephraim and Judea also broke the agreement and lost their place in the land—they were taken to Assyria and Babylon in the exile. Adam had to leave the garden and live among the Ubaid population who worked hard cultivating barley and wheat to make bread. "In the sweat of thy face shalt thou eat bread" (Gen 3:19 KJV).

When God first started to create life on earth, the "life" started small. We have many fossils from those early days, and if we have fossils then it must mean the creature died. As "life" got bigger we have fossils for the larger life too, and if we have fossils then it means those creatures died too. God gives and God takes away, that's the rule; a rule that applies to humans too. However, each human has an opportunity to grasp eternal life.

This universe was never meant to last forever; it is slowly running down as entropy takes its toll. The Apostle Paul said, "Flesh and blood cannot inherit the kingdom of God" (1 Cor 15:50). It seems that humans were never meant to live in this universe forever. Even Adam was not going to live forever, as he needed to eat from the tree of life to do that.

Death is a part of the natural order and if it wasn't we would never learn the lesson that separation from God is death. He is the source of all life; we are to breathe the spiritual atmosphere that clings to his being. When the cells of our physical body fail to replicate our spirit will still be breathing that fine air from above. If we say that humanity should not die a physical death then we can also insist that neither should they sleep, both physical death and sleep are used to describe what happens to our bodies when they have served their term here on earth.

The universe is a school, our surroundings on earth are the classroom, and the Holy Spirit is our teacher. Our job is to apply ourselves and graduate by hearing those words, "Well done, good and faithful servant!" (Matt 25:23).

Chapter 22
Faith

GOD BEGAN A CHAIN of events with Adam that would lead to the birth of God's son Jesus and consequently the salvation of all who put their trust in him.

Faith is of paramount importance. "Without faith it is impossible to please God" (Heb 11:6). Put simply, faith in Christ removes the spot and blemish prevalent in humanity. If we try to please God while still in our sins, we will fail. Sin is the reason God has removed himself from us, so trying to please God through any means, except the one he has prescribed, will end in failure.

We see our own derelict destitution through examples in the Bible. Jacob, the cheat and deceiver, ran away from home because his brother Esau wanted to kill him. Jacob, adrift in the open air, placed his head on a hard rock to sleep, probably feeling destitute and lying between a "rock and a hard place," yet it was at that point that God came to reveal himself to Jacob with a dream about a stairway to heaven. Samson, a judge in Israel, killed 30 men and stole their tunics to pay off a betting debt. He got into trouble with women and yet God used him, placing his Spirit upon Samson to execute judgement on Israel's enemies. King David committed adultery and attempted to cover his tracks with murder. The Bible is littered with examples of human beings falling short and yet God comes to our aid and often comes to rescue us at our lowest point. The first step in our liberation requires that each human being accept that we are indeed sinners and that we have no way of saving ourselves. We try hard not to sin but there seems to be a law within us that we are unable to overcome—the law of sin and death. The spirit is willing but the flesh truly is weak. No wonder the Apostle Paul cried out, "Wretched man that I am! Who will set me free from the body of this death?" (Rom 7:24 NASB). If we hold on to our pride we are lost, but if we throw ourselves on God's grace and mercy we will be saved.

God's desire is to rescue us because, though we are blighted, we still have his image upon us, we are still able to create because God is a creator. People procreate other people all the time, through socially acceptable channels or not, the human population continues to grow. We also create art, music, great architecture, fine cuisine, and beautiful clothes to wear, but when we place our faith in Christ we find that other channels of creativity are suddenly open to us: through prayer our creativity begins to blossom, we can affect and change the universe around us by praying with faith. We sometimes have a request in prayer, but little known to us, the chain of events required for the request to be answered needed to be set in motion before we prayed.

Imagine a mother praying for her son to be kept safe on his walking vacation through the mountains. God hears the mother's prayer but knows that the son is walking in an area where rocks have a tendency to dislodge and hurtle down the mountainside. Sure enough, as the mother's son is walking along a particular hazardous area a rock does in fact dislodge and falls, rolling and tumbling with some force down the steep descent, the rock seems to onlookers to be heading straight for the mother's son. But because the shape of the mountain changes slightly above where the young man is walking the rock narrowly misses him. He breathed a sigh of relief when he realized how close he had come to disaster. The mother thanks the Lord when she hears of her son's narrow escape. The mother's neighbor has no faith in God and he says, "It was a lucky escape for the boy and nothing more." But the mother cannot be convinced of that. The neighbor explains that the contour of the mountainside has been shaped over many years and the trajectory of the rock was just so that it just happened to miss the boy. The mother believes that God who made the mountain and the rock knew that she would pray and designed the circumstances to accommodate her prayer. Jesus taught us that "Your Father knows what you need before you ask him." God hears our prayer before we have prayed it, and he can set in place the providential circumstances needed for our prayer to be answered before we prayed, perhaps long before we prayed. Our prayers help to shape the universe around us in more ways than one.

Before they call I will answer. (Isa 65:24)

Faith

We can easily underestimate the power of faith. Faith in Christ will save our souls. The center of our being is able to choose. Our ability to choose is what separates us from the animal kingdom. The message of Jesus (and John the Baptist) was, "Repent, for the kingdom of heaven has come near" (Matt 3:2). The word "repent" means to rethink. The "re" means to turn or change and the "pent" relates to our mind. If we are "pensive" we are thoughtful. In French the word "think" is *penser* and in Spanish it is *pensar*. What we think is powerful and we choose what to think. Spirit is central to a human being, it gives us the ability to choose. Our "spirit" has been given to us by God when we were made in his image, it is that intangible part of us that enables us to think creative thoughts, spirit gives rise to our consciousness (and our conscience).

Human beings have always seemed to know that we have "spirit," that's one reason why there have been so many religions throughout human history, but perhaps it is only in the last hundred years that quantum physicists have been able to quantify how important human consciousness is. The famous double slit experiment of 1927 revealed that human observation affects the outcome of a particle either being a wave or a physical object; revealing the significance of human consciousness. John Wheeler's delayed choice quantum experiment reveals that simply observing subatomic particles not only causes them to exist, but also causes them to have existed prior to observation. While physicists and philosophers continue to debate how data from these experiments relates to the universe around us the Bible itself agrees with the results of the quantum experiments, telling us that our thoughts and faith have far reaching implications.

Eminent American quantum physicist John Wheeler who worked on human consciousness revealed that human consciousness alone seems to shape not only the present but the past as well. Wheeler, a scientist and colleague of Albert Einstein and mentor to many leading physicists, and the man who chose the name "black hole" to describe the collapse of a large star under the force of gravity, said, "Every item of the physical world has at bottom . . . an immaterial source."[1] Each human being has his or her part to play in the creation of the universe. As Wheeler said, "This is a participatory universe."[2]

These are hard concepts to grasp but once understood reveal to the Christian just how strong and far reaching faith is—faith in Christ counts.

---

1. Wheeler, "Information, Physics, Quantum," 311.
2. Ibid.

God and Primordial People

We are made in God's image and have our own ability to create, realizing this enables us to see that when we fail to fall in line with God's goodness he takes his guiding hand away from us and "gives us over" to our own creative mayhem. We create our own sinfulness. We have our own part to play in creation, leading to the consequence that we have our own part to play in being "given over." Paul pointed out in Romans 1 that God has to take his hands off us and gives us over to our own devices. But it is not only Paul who asserts this:

- Psalm 81:12 states, "So I gave them over to their stubborn hearts."
- Stephen in Acts 7:42 says, "God turned away from them and gave them over to the worship of the sun, moon and stars."
- Isaiah declares, "you have hidden your face from us and have given us over to our sins" (Isa 64:7).

Faith in Christ redeems and rescues us from our own sinfulness. Human consciousness helps to shape the world around us, for ill or for good. That is why repenting, changing our mind, is so important. Jeremiah wondered, *could a leopard change its spots?* He concluded that it could not and said, "Neither can you do good who are accustomed to doing evil" (Jer 13:23): this is the plight in which we find ourselves. A leopard may not be able to change its spots but the spot that we are afflicted with can be erased by faith in Jesus Christ, when we repent and change our way of thinking. "Let God transform you inwardly by a complete change of your mind" (Rom 12:2 GNT). "Therefore, if anyone is in Christ, he is a new creature; the old things passed away; behold, new things have come" (2 Cor 5:17 NASB).

Faith is what carries weight here. We have the "sinner's prayer" and "Alpha Courses" and "Journey into Life" booklets, etc., and all of these are good, but they are only good because they lead to faith. When the friends of a paralyzed man lowered their disabled friend through the roof of a house to reach Jesus, the first thing Jesus said to the disabled man when he saw the incident was, "Friend, your sins are forgiven" (Luke 5:20). The bedridden man had no counseling, he did not say the sinner's prayer and yet his sins were forgiven simply by placing his faith in Jesus.

Chapter 23
Bad from Birth

Surely I was sinful at birth, sinful from the time my mother conceived me. (Ps 51:5)

AFTER MAN BEGAN TO steer his own selfish course and consequently modify his own being as a result, God began to make provision for man's rescue. The plan of salvation saw its first practical steps with Adam and Eve whose offspring would lead to Christ being born. God used Adam as an example by highlighting our waywardness with the simple command for Adam and Eve not to eat from the tree of the knowledge of good and evil, a command they were unable to keep. During the ensuing years, on the way to Christ's birth, God began to teach humanity the correct way to live. Formerly we needed no teaching because the law of God was in our hearts.

In the early books of the Bible we can see God's determination to teach us his ways. In the book of Exodus the young nation of Israel is taught by God in the Sinai wilderness to live one day at a time—which was of course the way we used to live in humanity's primeval days. God fed the Israelites daily with bread from heaven, engendering simple trust in their hearts. If any of the Israelites gathered more manna than they needed for that particular day the surplus would not last until tomorrow, it would rot. Jesus also took time to teach us to live daily by faith in God. When we worry we become a modern replica of the Israelites trying to store up manna for tomorrow just in case God doesn't provide for us. Lack of faith facilitates worry, stress, and frustration, and those negative attributes are all constituent parts of our fallen nature. But faith dispels fear. Simple trust gives us a pattern for a peaceful, blessed, adventurous, and fulfilled life.

Though human beings have been "given over," or as explained in Ephesians, "given themselves over," having faith changes our being.

> Having lost all sensitivity, they have given themselves over to sensuality so as to indulge in every kind of impurity, and they are full of greed. That, however, is not the way of life you learned when you heard about Christ and were taught in him in accordance with the truth that is in Jesus. You were taught, with regard to your former way of life, to put off your old self, which is being corrupted by its deceitful desires; to be made new in the attitude of your minds; and to put on the new self, created to be like God in true righteousness and holiness. (Eph 4:19–24)

"If anyone is in Christ, he is a new creature" (2 Cor 5:17). The Bible explains:

- The state we are in.
- How we got there.
- The escape route provided for us.

Genesis chapter 1 recounts God's majestic creation and finishes its last verse with "God saw all that he had made, and it was very good." However, humanity did not play its part in the "goodness" of creation. We were made in God's image but we used our own ability to create for ill means. We constructed an evil path to walk. We failed to maintain the soundness in which we had been made and therefore the integrity of our being suffered. The spiritual poison injected by the serpent into humankind spread throughout the Homo sapient population, not unlike a disease can spread throughout a close-knit community.

What happened to the Neanderthals or Homo erectus or any other member of the hominid family we are unable to say. Some were undoubtedly merely animal but others may not have been. But as the only surviving member of the genus Homo, the Bible informs us that Homo sapiens, or what we know as modern humans, are presently born with a spot and blemish that was not in God's original design for us.

> Even from birth the wicked go astray; from the womb they are wayward, spreading lies. Their venom is like the venom of a snake, like that of a cobra that has stopped its ears, that will not heed the tune of the charmer, however skillful the enchanter may be. (Ps 58:3–4)

The evil within the Homo sapient population did not bode well for other members of the genus Homo. One possibility is that God saw fit to allow the other members to die out because of the risk that they would be ill used by the corrupt Homo sapiens—our modern-day police force will be quick to clear an area of people if there is a chance that some of them may get hurt by a terrorist threat. Perhaps Homo sapiens posed a threat to other members of the genus Homo.

Our modern human ancestors first journeyed from the African continent around 50,000 to 60,000 years ago. During that period we know of two other hominid species living on earth, the Neanderthals and Denisovans. We may be misled by comic book portrayals of obtuse thick-skulled Neanderthals; archaeologists have known for some time that the Neanderthal people were adept at controlling fire. Recent studies of Neanderthal remains reveal that this archaic group cooked and ate plants and vegetables. Researchers in the United States have found grains of cooked plant material in the teeth of Neanderthal remains. "Neandertals are often portrayed as very backwards or primitive," said Amanda Henry, lead researcher in the Center for the Advanced Study of Human Paleobiology. "Now we are beginning to understand that they had some quite advanced technologies and behaviors."[1]

When the modern humans traveled northwards they encountered the Neanderthals and (unsurprisingly) it seems that some interbreeding took place; subsequently people who now live outside of Africa possess a small percentage of Neanderthal DNA. Scientists who have analyzed the genomes of modern humans and Neanderthals say the results indicate that many European people and also those living in Asia have 1 to 2 percent Neanderthal DNA. And yet sub-Saharan Africans possess either none or an extremely small amount. The reason seems to be the irresistible answer that their ancestors did not migrate northwards.

There is a mystery that surrounds the extinction of the Neanderthals, no one seems to be sure why they suddenly seem to disappear after thriving for many millennia. The departure of the Neanderthals fits the timing well—Homo sapiens are given over to their misdeeds and start to make images and worship pseudo deities at the same time the Neanderthals take their leave of planet earth. If the reason was God wanting to spare the Neanderthals pain, abuse, and perhaps even their own fall from grace, then Isaiah's words have a larger context than we may first appreciate.

1. CASHP, "Neandertals Had Varied Diet," para. 2.

God and Primordial People

> The righteous perish, and no one takes it to heart; the devout are taken away, and no one understands that the righteous are taken away to be spared from evil. Those who walk uprightly enter into peace; they find rest as they lie in death. (Isa 57:1–2)

Life for Homo sapiens certainly took a turn for the worse. Our fall meant we did not hit the ground running but landed heavily and awkwardly, injuring ourselves in the process. This turn of events allows for the possibility that the other members of the genus Homo, living on earth at that time, may also have been hurt from the fallout.

We may find ourselves wondering at the reason why the fall of humanity was so comprehensive, and spread throughout the whole community of Homo sapiens. The scenario in and around the garden of Eden reveals information placed there to help us understand. God often speaks through drama in the Bible, therefore when we see the woman eat the fruit of the tree of the knowledge of good and evil we understand that she is making use of a supposed hidden shortcut that the enemy made known to her. She could get wisdom fast and learn how to use "good and evil" for her own advantage. The people of primordial humanity who chose to take Satan's fast-track route found they were "given over" to behavior that used knowledge, craft, cunning, and intrigue to their own advantage. The Apostle Paul says they became "filled with every kind of wickedness, evil, greed and depravity. They are full of envy, murder, strife, deceit and malice . . . no fidelity, no love, no mercy" (Rom 1:29, 31). So we can presume that any modern humans who remained in the innocent state that God had made them were dispensed with through the intrigue, murder, and wickedness of fallen humanity. Cain murdering his brother Abel may depict this scenario well. The fall of humankind became complete until there was "no one righteous, not even one" (Rom 3:10).

Jeremiah diagnoses our malady. "This is what the Lord says: 'Your wound is incurable, your injury beyond healing. There is no one to plead your cause, no remedy for your sore, no healing for you. . . . Why do you cry out over your wound, your pain that has no cure? . . . But I will restore you to health and heal your wounds,'" (Jer 30:12–17). Yes, we are wounded beyond anyone's help save God.

We saw earlier how idols were the first archaeological indication of our fall. Any former hominids who enjoyed the simple life were better off escaping the intrigues of the wayward Homo sapiens. Isaiah continues,

Bad from Birth

> But you—come here, you children of a sorceress, you offspring of adulterers and prostitutes! Who are you mocking? At whom do you sneer and stick out your tongue? Are you not a brood of rebels, the offspring of liars? You burn with lust among the oaks and under every spreading tree; you sacrifice your children in the ravines and under the overhanging crags. The idols among the smooth stones of the ravines are your portion; indeed, they are your lot. (Isa 57:3–6)

Genesis chapter 2 moves us on to the location of southern Mesopotamia where God provides a generous supply of fresh water delivered by four primary rivers to a dry barren landscape. Once fresh water was in reach men took up residence there, digging irrigation channels and growing crops. God planted a garden there, and placed a man in the garden through whom he would begin a chain of generations leading to the Savior of the world being born.

Adam—the man in the garden—took on the name of men and represented men in the scenario we see in the garden of Eden. The local Sumerian people have their own records of what happened in those days. The Sumerian language has no modern equivalent language, unlike Akkadian, so we will not always see a connection in the Sumerian words or names they used. The Bible teaches us that Cain built a city, the name of the city was Enoch named after Cain's son. The city of Eridu was another southern Mesopotamian city and appears to be the city in which Adam and Eve lived after their employment in the garden of Eden had been terminated. The Sumerian King List describes Eridu as the first city in the southern Mesopotamian area that had a king. God breathed into Adam in 5148 BC (according to Septuagint numbers; see appendix A). Eridu was already a small community by the time Adam took his place within it, and as a result of his long years was soon recognized as a leader of men, as were his offspring.

Cain was told by Yahweh to remove himself entirely from the locality because he had been found guilty of murder. Information is sparse regarding Cain and so some speculation is required but we may be able to piece together certain aspects of Cain's life, city, and his offspring.

The city of what we now know as Uruk started sometime before 4000 BC. According to the Sumerian King List, Mesh-ki-ang-gasher was the city's first ruler and the man under whom it was built. Uruk is a strong contender for the city that Cain built. There is no biblical record of the birth of Cain so we can't reliably date it, but his younger brother Seth was born in 4918 BC. The majority of Adam's antediluvian male offspring fathered children before they reached the age of 200, including four of them who were in their 160s when they first became fathers. Adam is slightly out of line as he was 230 before Seth was born, but that is because Adam had already fathered two boys, Cain and Abel. So, let us say that Adam could father children around the age of 160, Cain and Abel seem to have been born in quick succession, Cain would be born around 4988 BC, so by the time he was 68 years old in 4920 BC he killed his younger brother. Cain was young in relative terms and Abel was slightly younger. Cain could not yet father children because it wasn't until he had left the area and started his building project that he fathered his son Enoch. The elongated childhood of Adam and his antediluvian offspring can probably be seen in Cain for two reasons. The first is that Cain was not sentenced to death for his crime of murder, some leniency can be seen in his sentence that may have been extended to him because of his age. He was 68, and in a regular lifespan that would be old, but for Cain it meant that he was probably emerging out of childhood. He was a rebellious youth who learned a hard lesson—we also show leniency in the modern world with youths who commit crime and are not punished as severely as adults would be because they are young. Secondly, we can see the childhood/adolescent phase in Cain's reply to Yahweh when he said, "Am I my brother's keeper?" indicating that his brother had a "keeper." Let's remember that the scribe from Lagash appears to ridicule the long-livers by pointing out they were children in diapers for a long time, and not only were they slow to grow up they were also dull-witted, and needed someone to watch over them, usually the mother. At the time of Abel's murder Cain appears to have emerged from the childhood stage but was not yet able to father children.

God helped Adam and Eve replace Abel with Seth, and not too long after his death. Eve said, "God has granted me another child in place of Abel, since Cain killed him" (Gen 4:25). God was keen to see the line to Christ continue. Adam and his male successors, in the nine generations before Noah, fathered their first-born male at ages between approximately 160 and 200. The earliest community settlements found in Uruk are what archaeologists call Uruk XVIII dating back to around 5000 BC. But these early settlements were not a city and are still considered as part of the Ubaid period. Cain, it seems, made his way to these settlements for reasons of daily food, shelter, and finding a wife. Let us say that Cain could father children around the age of 180 taking us to the year 4808 BC when Cain's son Enoch was born.

Bad from Birth

> Cain had relations with his wife and she conceived, and gave birth to Enoch; and he built a city, and called the name of the city Enoch, after the name of his son. (Gen 4:17 NASB)

Building a city takes time and Cain had the time far above that of regular human beings. The Sumerian King List states that the builder of Uruk was Mesh-ki-ang-gasher the son of Utu. The Sumerian language may have pronounced Adam's name as Utu and Cain as Mesh-ki-ang-gasher, if so Cain's son Enoch would be pronounced Enmerkar, who was the son of Mesh-ki-ang-gasher. Both Enmerkar and Enoch have the Sumerian prefix "En," meaning "ruler" or "lord." And Mesh-ki-ang-gasher seems to have a literary resemblance to Cain in its middle. Ki in the Sumerian language seems to mean "earth," and we know that Cain worked the land or earth. Seth named his son "Enosh," again using the Sumerian prefix "En." The Sumerian language died out but their Akkadian neighbors' language grew and developed into several modern languages. Adam and his near offspring may have spoken some Sumerian, hence En became a prefix in those early years but then disappeared as Akkadian became the predominant language. Akkadian words eventually gave rise to the Hebrew language, among other languages, and although the Akkadian and Sumerian scribes both used cuneiform to record their words, their languages were unrelated.

The Sumerian King List gives us the approximate year that Uruk became a recognized city as 4544 BC. Cain's son Enoch would then be 264, relating to approximately 26 years old in our terms. The Sumerian King List also mentions that Mesh-ki-ang-gasher (Cain) seems to disappear and may have drowned in the sea. Cain does not have the honor of having his own toledoth in the book of Genesis but we do read of his posterity up to six generations. Genesis mentions that Cain's sixth generation included Tubal-Cain, who forged all kinds of tools out of bronze and iron. The city of Uruk was well on its feet by the time Tubal-Cain was working with metal. The Bronze Age in the Near East began with the rise of Sumer in the fourth millennium BC. The Neolithic Period had now finished and the Bronze Age had begun. From Tubal-Cain's name, we may get the ancient god Vulcan. The omission of the Tu leaves us with Bal-Cain and by turning the b into v, a change sometimes made by the Hebrews, Greeks, and Romans, we are left with Vulcan, the god of metalworking, fire, and forge.

When we read the history of southern Mesopotamia we will not read too far before we come across the goddess Inanna, the most prominent female deity of the area. Inanna was associated with the city of Uruk. Inanna

God and Primordial People

was the goddess of love, sensuality, fertility, procreation, and the Akkadians called her "Ishtar." She was the Phoenician "Astarte" and the Greek "Aphrodite." Inanna was also compared to the bright planet Venus, who we know in Roman mythology was the goddess of love. These other names for Inanna reveal her stunning beauty and sensuality. Inanna seems to be characterized as a youthful female, not as a maternal mature woman or faithful wife. She understands her power and uses it to her full advantage. In the Mesopotamian story "The Epic of Gilgamesh" Ishtar (Inanna) attempts to seduce Gilgamesh, but he, being aware of her history as a sexual predator, reminds Ishtar how her former lovers have met with various calamities once she had discarded them, and he does not want to be among their number. The Venerable Bede (born in AD 673) speaks of a goddess who was celebrated in the Old English "Month of Ēostre," a month corresponding to April, which he says, "was once called after a goddess named Ēostre." The Phoenician "Astarte" may be a match for what the Venerable Bede was speaking of, if so, we seem to get our word modern "Easter" from Ishtar.

We know that Adam and Eve's female offspring were attractive. "The sons of God saw that the daughters of men were beautiful" (Gen 6:2 NASB). The word "men" in Hebrew is Adam. So in Hebrew the verse would read, "The sons of God saw that the daughters of Adam were beautiful." We see the "beauty" trait throughout Adam's later offspring: Sarah, "I know what a beautiful woman you are" (12:11), Rebekah "was very beautiful" (24:16), and "Rachel was beautiful in form and appearance" (29:17). So it is probable that Cain's offspring were also beautiful. Cain's genealogical line ends with naming "Tubal-Cain's sister as Naamah" (4:22), which makes us wonder, *why is Naamah mentioned?* Her brothers all seem to have important jobs, we see that Jabal raised livestock and was an authority on sojourning with tents, Jubal was a master musician, and Tubal-Cain had his metalwork, so for what reason is Naamah listed? Females did not often make it into biblical genealogical records unless there was some reason of note.

Naamah means "pleasant," as in "pleasing to the eye." We suppose that Moses thought it worthwhile recording Naamah's name because we would be aware of her. Naamah herself held onto her beauty for many years because she was from a line that lives long. Men of that era, with a regular lifespan, would see themselves grow older while Naamah appeared to remain in the prime of her youth. Stories, legends, and myths would not be in short supply when Naamah finally died, succeeding generations would tell stories that they had heard about a beautiful woman who held onto her looks while many around her lost theirs.

The city of Uruk was a formidable towering presence in early Bronze Age Mesopotamia, and began to fill the area with its mass-produced wares, that were noticeably of a lesser quality to the fine standard of pottery that Eridu and other areas had taken time and craftsmanship to produce. Cain's family seemed to have taken the city on a particular course that Yahweh, or the surrounding people, would not appreciate.

The surrounding Ubaid people were thoughtful in their craftsmanship; they designed their rectangular temple buildings to align with the cardinal points of the compass. The earliest temple at Eridu was found to have a simple offering table or altar. Adam's son Abel offered some of the firstborn of his flock as an offering (perhaps on that table), which pleased Yahweh. Cain brought some fruit of his crops to offer, which didn't please Yahweh. Josephus remarks that Cain brought the fruits of the earth offering the work of his husbandry but Abel brought first-fruits of his flocks, and God was more delighted with Abel's offering because he offered what grew naturally of its own accord, while Cain's offering was an invention of man obtained by forcing the ground.

Perhaps with Cain and Abel we see the two diametrically opposed lifestyles that existed between the "natural" state that God created us in and the "paradise lost" state of the later manufactured cultivation designed by humanity. Cultivating the soil and "forcing the ground" was not what God had originally intended, nevertheless Cain and his offspring played their part with gusto. Abel, on the other hand, worked with the animals that humans were told to dominate back in Genesis chapter 1. In the offerings of Cain and Abel we may also see that without the shedding of blood there is no remission of sins (Heb 9:22).

When Adam was told to leave the garden of Eden, God said, "Cursed is the ground for thy sake; in sorrow shalt thou eat of it all the days of thy life . . . and thou shalt eat the herb of the field; In the sweat of thy face shalt thou eat bread" (Gen 3:17–19 KJV). The land that had previously been amply supplied by four rivers began to lose its abundant supply of water. Two of the rivers, the Pishon and Gihon, dried up completely. Adam, and the local people living in the area, would have to work hard to cultivate their crops—digging irrigation channels that included a regular maintenance schedule to avoid the silting-up process would be a major part of cultivating wheat, barley, and other crops.

God and Primordial People

One mistake that is easy for us modern readers of the book of Genesis to make is when we get phrases like, "And the whole earth was of one language, and of one speech" (Gen 11:1 KJV). We need to remember that what the modern mind views as the whole earth and the ancient Mesopotamian mind views as the whole earth will be completely different. The modern mind has knowledge of planet earth as a globe orbiting the sun in space. We have globes sitting on desks where we can plainly see the seven continents—Africa, Antarctica, Asia, Australia/Oceania, Europe, North America, and South America. We also have the countries of each continent all neatly and accurately mapped out for us, so when we say "the whole earth" we know exactly what we mean. The ancient man living by the river Euphrates or the river Nile did not have access to all that information, much of the world outside the Fertile Crescent was unknown and therefore mysterious. What he meant by the whole earth encompassed only the people groups he knew of.

Two thousand years after the time that Genesis chapter 11 tells us about, we see another example where people had still not got the full picture of what planet earth was comprised of. In Luke 2 verse 1 we read, "And it came to pass in those days, that there went out a decree from Caesar Augustus, that all the world should be taxed." That is how the King James Version phrases the verse, and the wording is faithful to Luke's Greek manuscript. However, we know from historical records that Caesar Augustus did not have any jurisdiction over countries like China, who at that time had a nine-year-old male by the name of Ping of Han as emperor. There were numerous countries that were not under Roman rule. South America had tribal chiefdoms called the Nazca culture, existing between 100 BC and AD 800, and these chiefdoms were not affected by the decree sent out by Caesar Augustus. Many other countries of the world were unaffected, far too many for me to mention. That is why some modern translations of the Bible add a word to Luke 2:1 that is not in the Greek manuscript, and the word they add is "Roman." The NIV says, "In those days Caesar Augustus issued a decree that a census should be taken of the entire Roman world." This enables the modern man or woman to grasp what the Bible means when they read in Genesis 11:1 "the whole earth," the phrase needs to be put into context of the life and times of the Mesopotamian culture of that day.

After Adam's expulsion from the garden of fruit trees, the rivers in southern Mesopotamia did not flow as they once did, thus affecting the local cultivation of crops, making the work considerably harder. When Noah was born his father named him Noah saying, "He will comfort us in the labor and painful toil of our hands caused by the ground the LORD has cursed" (Gen 5:29). Noah means "rest or comfort." Lamech, Noah's father, was still living in southern Mesopotamia and in his days the water sanctions had started to bite, consequently the agriculture suffered. Adam and his cohorts would be allowed to "plow the fields and scatter the good seed on the ground" but the process would be harsh and ultimately sweaty hard work. A diminished water supply meant that land left to itself would tend towards weeds that must be removed and also a network of irrigation channels needed to be dug to compensate for the two rivers that had dried up. The Epic of Gilgamesh written in southern Mesopotamia and dating to around 2100 BC speaks of "thistles" and the "dark prick-thorn," allowing us to see that Mesopotamians were aware of thistles and thorns.

Psalm 107 paints a picture for us of what happened in those early days of human civilization. The artistic form of the Psalm paints a series of vivid pictures and one particular illustration begins at verse 33 (KJV), "He turneth rivers into a wilderness, and the watersprings into dry ground." The psalm continues with verse 34, "A fruitful land into barrenness, for the wickedness of them that dwell therein." The scene portrayed for us in Genesis chapter 2 of southern Mesopotamia boasts of a land with an abundant supply of fresh water, hence the sudden growth in population around 6000 BC to 5000 BC. But because two of the rivers ran dry, we can suppose that the water supply was cut by up to 50 percent, having a huge impact on the agriculture of the area. This impact was a result of Adam's unwillingness to follow Yahweh's command along with the violence and commercialism of Cain's family members and also, let us not forget, the infiltration of the human gene pool, "when the sons of God went to the daughters of humans and had children by them" (Gen 6:4). So the verdant land was turned into a desert. Looking at the area of Eridu these days, it is hard to imagine that the area was once so productive. Psalm 107 continues in verse 35 by explaining that not only is God able to reduce the supply of water to a specified area he is also able to boost it, for he "turned the desert into pools of water and the parched ground into flowing springs; there he brought the hungry to live." We are being told the story of Abraham's family who left southern Mesopotamia for Canaan. Abram and his nephew Lot viewed the land to where they had recently journeyed and Lot in particular noticed that "the whole plain of the Jordan toward Zoar was well watered, like the garden of the Lord" (Gen 13:10).

Chapter 24
Bone and Flesh

> Put your hand under my thigh. I want you to swear by the Lord, the God of heaven and the God of earth, that you will not get a wife for my son from the daughters of the Canaanites, among whom I am living, but will go to my country and my own relatives and get a wife for my son Isaac. (Gen 24:2–4)

ABRAHAM'S IMPASSIONED PLEA TO his servant discloses information that has important contextual value. If we consider that Abraham married again after the death of Sarah, without a long journey back to Mesopotamia being recorded, we are left to conclude that Abraham's wife Keturah was a local girl. The genetic line to Christ was being made through Abraham and Sarah's offspring, Isaac. Sarah was Abraham's half sister, preserving the close familial bond that seems to be needed to preserve the DNA first administered to Adam, and then through Adam's stem cells to Eve. Perhaps that is why we read of the Israelites' strict guidelines for marriage. When Ezra heard that the Israelites had "taken some of their daughters as wives for themselves and their sons, and have mingled the holy race with the peoples around them. And the leaders and officials have led the way in this unfaithfulness," he said, "I tore my tunic and cloak, pulled hair from my head and beard and sat down appalled" (Ezra 9:2–3). Once Abraham had faithfully discharged the duty of getting a wife for his son Isaac from one of his close family members, thereby continuing the line to Christ, Abraham himself was then free and able to marry a local girl, because he was under no restriction to preserve the genetic line to Christ that God was watching over with enthusiastic keenness. Abraham's close relationship to Yahweh had yielded the information that Abraham passed on to his servant about the importance of where Isaac was to find a wife.

The fruit of Abraham and Keturah's relationship included six boys, (probably some girls too). One boy, Midian, became the father of the Midianites. A few generations later Moses married Zipporah who was a part of the Midianite nation. Abraham sent his and Keturah's six male offspring eastwards and away from his son Isaac, so the likelihood of Isaac's offspring mating with Abraham and Keturah's offspring was slim. The six sons of Abraham and Keturah were not in the line to Christ, although Moses married a Midianite he was from the tribe of Levi and not Judah, the tribe that contained the line to Christ. In Numbers 25 verse 6 we see an Israelite man executed because he brought a Midianite woman into the Israelite camp just prior to their conquest of Canaan. So the zeal and care with which Abraham chose a wife for Isaac was not repeated when he chose a wife for himself after Sarah's death. His part in securing the path through to Christ had been completed with Isaac and Rebekah, who were close relatives to each other.

Adam's wife had been made from one of his rib bones. This, of course, is unlike any other means of female generation. Adam's close family members were aware of it. Cain left the clan and seems to have married a local woman from the Ubaid culture, thus losing his close family's heritage. Cain may have seen this as having certain advantages regarding the education of his children, who would have less years of childhood and be quicker to learn than his brother Seth's children. The enhanced pace of learning for Cain's clan would be offset by a shorter overall lifespan. Adam's family would naturally fragment and go their separate ways, but Yahweh was watching over the line from Adam's family that would lead to the birth of his son. "When the Most High divided the nations, when he separated the sons of Adam, he set the bounds of the nations according to the number of the angels of God. And his people Jacob became the portion of the Lord, Israel was the line of his inheritance" (Deut 32:8–9 LXX).

We see the line's closeness when they greet each other with the phrase, "Surely you are my bone and my flesh" (Gen 29:14 NASB). Some translations of the Bible go for the "flesh and blood" option here that seems to make more sense to us in the modern world. Indeed, "flesh and blood" is a theme that Christians are familiar with because we are told that the body and blood of Christ are represented by the bread and wine of communion. Jesus himself taught us that "unless you eat the flesh of the Son of Man and drink his blood, you have no life in you" (John 6:53). The Christian family relates to the phrase "flesh and blood" as do most other families. "Flesh and blood" is a familiar New Testament phrase, but back in the early days of which the Old Testament speaks, we find that Adam first spoke of bone of my bones and flesh of my flesh to Eve. From that point on, certain families were able to say that phrase too, but not all families. When the men of Israel approached David in the hope he would agree to be their king they appealed to David's sense of family. "Then all the tribes of Israel came to David at Hebron and said, "Behold, we are your bone and your flesh" (2 Sam 5:1). David was in the line to Christ.

When Christ was born John tells us, "He came to that which was his own, but his own did not receive him" (John 1:11). Not all men can say they are of Adam's bone and flesh, we know that humans have inhabited planet earth for millennia before Adam and Eve had children. God chose Adam to begin the line to Christ by taking a man, breathing into him in a special way that changed his regular lifespan and also added other attributes. God began his own family on earth. We are all of the same flesh as Adam, but Eve became the mother of the line that would lead to Christ—"The mother of all living" (Gen 3:20 KJV). Through Christ we find ourselves no longer "dead in trespasses and sins" (Eph 2:1) but "alive to God in Christ Jesus" (Rom 6:11). Eve becomes our mother too because we are now "living" in Christ.

Life and death are the important points that scripture asserts, but the words are referencing life and death from an eternal perspective. Scripture also speaks of our "heart" not meaning our physical heart, and we also read of "light and darkness" not meaning photons or the lack of them, the Bible is referring to the light of God, which is far more than mere physical light. Indeed, the light we see in this universe is there to represent the light of God. The same applies to "life and death." Physical bodies die and always have, but God uses physical life and death to teach us about "The Life." Jesus said, "I am . . . the life" (John 14:6). We have to take care that current popular doctrines don't infiltrate the truth of the Bible, and "death entering the world after the disobedience of Adam in the garden" is dogma that has entered into some quarters of the church. Even Bible translators can be pulled into interpreting, and consequently translating, the Bible in the light of their church's doctrine rather than what is actually written. For instance in Romans 8:10 the NIV (copyright 2011) translates the verse as, "if Christ is in you, then even though your body is subject to death because of sin." The phrase "subject to death" gives us the feel that "Yes, our bodies are alive but one day they will die." But the King James Version follows the Greek text carefully by translating the same verse as, "if Christ be in you, the body is dead because of sin." The New American Standard Bible also follows the "formal equivalence" method of translation used by the translators of the KJV and vigilantly translates this verse as, "the body is dead because of sin." We see that Paul actually wrote that our bodies are dead. They are dead now, not at some point in the future. Sin has destroyed them for the "life of God." The only way we can now receive "life" is by faith in Christ. "The Spirit gives life; the flesh counts for nothing" (John 6:63). Men have always died, our physical life is there for the same reason that anything else in this universe was created: to teach us about spiritual life and enable us to choose that life.

So when Christ came to "his own" the text is directing us back to Adam and Eve who were bone and flesh of Christ. The fact that Luke highlights the genealogical line all the way back to Adam shows us that Adam most probably wasn't the first Homo sapien. Otherwise there's no need to highlight the line all the way back to Adam. (But if we want to read it that way and stay true to what we know from science then we can do so by taking Luke's genealogy back to Adam in the garden and then remembering that Adam was taken from "Adam" [plural] and took their name upon himself, hence representing Homo sapiens.) If Adam the man is the progenitor of the whole human race then there is no need to mention that Christ's line goes all the way back to Adam because everyone's line goes all the way back to Adam, so why mention it in the first place? Matthew's genealogy of Jesus doesn't go any further back than Abraham. Luke could have followed Matthew's example because scholars tell us that Matthew's gospel was written before Luke's gospel. Going all the way to Adam seems superfluous if everyone's genealogical line ends with Adam. But if Adam was chosen as a representative human and God breathed into him in some special way, and made a woman from his rib so that the generating of this couple would lead eventually to Christ's birth, then Luke would have every reason to mention the line all the way back to Adam. Paul in Romans 9:3–5 explains that to "his race, the people of Israel . . . belongs the human ancestry of Christ . . . traced through the fathers," i.e., son of David, son of Abraham, son of Adam, all of whom were fathers in the line to Christ. Adam means "man"— Christ is the Son of man.

Isaiah points out that it is Jacob's ancestry that comes from Adam. "You have not called on me, Jacob" (Isa 43:22) and "Your first forefather sinned" (27). Jacob's people were Christ's "own." A little later Isaiah mentions that it is Israel who was established from ancient times. "I established my ancient people" (44:7). God began the process with Adam and Eve in ancient times—bone of bone and flesh of flesh. "He came to that which was his own, but his own did not receive him" (John 1:11).

We took part in our own making; God granted us the ability to shape our own personalities, desires, and character, God was there to help guide and lead but we rejected his leading so he "gave us over" to our own devices. And since God has given us over to our "many schemes" our fall was made complete. Paul explains in Romans chapter 1 verses 28–31, "they did not think it worthwhile to retain the knowledge of God, so God gave them over to a depraved mind, so that they do what ought not to be done. They have become filled with every kind of wickedness, evil, greed and depravity. They are full of envy, murder, strife, deceit and malice. They are gossips, slanderers, God-haters, insolent, arrogant and boastful; they invent ways of doing evil; they disobey their parents; they have no understanding, no fidelity, no love, no mercy."

Chapter 25
The Work of Our Hands

A FEATURE OF BEING "made" in God's image and likeness is the ability humans have to also "make." We, ourselves, use God's likeness to make, in other words we create works of art, admirable architecture, lush landscape gardens, classy motor vehicles, stylish living rooms, emotive poetry, and evocative songs. The list is long and included in the list is our ability to shape our own being. We shape ourselves!

One way that we shape ourselves is by changing our physical frame. We alter our body by what we eat and the exercise we do. We can greatly change our physical shape for good or for ill. Another way that we can shape ourselves is by consistently doing good or consistently doing bad, either of which will undoubtedly forge the character that we slowly develop. How we habitually behave will become an elementary feature within our human makeup: an unchecked grudge can turn into hardened hatred, but a willingness to forgive can turn into a permanent generosity of spirit. God grants us this capacity to create ourselves, but he is, of course, willing to work with us, as a parent will help guide the hand of a young child when doing some task they are learning. But if the child is willful and continually pulls away from the parent's guiding hand, then the adult may leave the child to their own devices, leaving the child to "learn the hard way."

The universe we live in is the framework used to learn our craft of creating. Space and time is the infrastructure that God has set apart for us to shape ourselves. The material construct in which we presently exist is an area set aside by God where gaps may appear in the goodness, in other words "things can go wrong." In heaven, the area in which God makes his home, nothing is amiss or out of place or imperfect. Jesus highlighted this fact when he taught us to pray, "Let your will be done on earth as it is in

God and Primordial People

heaven." We have to pray this prayer because the request is needed—life on earth is not always as God would wish, his pleasing and perfect will is not always done on earth. When God "gave us over" to our sins, the time when we refused to be guided by his gracious parental hand, was the point in which our characters took a wrong turn by our own hand, we made ourselves into an imperfect product with a flawed nature, an evil mind, and a skewed sexuality. We cannot present to God a damaged, distorted, and defaced product; he will not receive it. Indeed the product we have created with our own blemished nature has no place in God's kingdom. Perfection alone resides in his precincts and that is why Uzzah died. "When they came to the threshing floor of Nakon, Uzzah reached out and took hold of the ark of God, because the oxen stumbled" (2 Sam 6:6). He immediately died. Imperfection has no place in the kingdom of heaven; it won't fit. Inadequate work will not get passed quality control.

When heaven comes near to earth, men need to take great care. God warned Moses to tell the Israelites, "Put limits for the people around the mountain and tell them, 'Be careful that you do not approach the mountain or touch the foot of it. Whoever touches the mountain is to be put to death'" (Exod 19:12). An ice cube cannot exist in a hot environment, and our cold hearts cannot break through into heaven. Isaiah cried out, "Woe is me, for I am ruined! Because I am a man of unclean lips, And I live among a people of unclean lips; For my eyes have seen the King, the LORD of hosts" (Isa 6:5). Samson's father bewailed his position by exclaiming, "We are doomed to die! We have seen God!" (Judg 13:32).

Moses, and the seventy elders with him, "saw the God of Israel; and under His feet there appeared to be a pavement of sapphire, as clear as the sky itself" (Exod 24:10 NASB). But the warning was issued, "do not let the priests and the people break through to come up to the LORD" (19:24 NASB). The seventy elders were allowed because they had been previously sprinkled with blood. Something had worked in their favor.

Cain offered the work of his hands to the LORD God, but his offering did not meet with divine approval. We presented ourselves—the work of our hands—to God through Christ, because Christ became human and was one of us. We said, "Here we are Lord, what do you think of what we have made with the work of our own hands?" And God replied through the prophet Jeremiah, "'You did not listen to me,' declares the LORD, 'and you have aroused my anger with what your hands have made, and you have brought harm to yourselves'" (Jer 25:7). So, in Christ, God was presented with what our own hands had made and God consequently showed us exactly what he thought of the work of our hands. Christ's body was broken, pummelled, whipped, pierced, and finally killed. That is what God thought of what our own hands have made, our offering was only fit to be smashed.

When God created the universe he saw that "it was good" but we have created in our own person something that is bad. The badness must be demolished and Christ took on humanity so that what we have made could be destroyed. Jesus Christ destroyed the sinful nature on our behalf. But that is not the end of the story, praise God! Christ did not stay in his grave, he rose again, and he passes on that new life to anyone who, by faith, will receive his resurrection life. Therefore, if anyone is in Christ, he is a new creation. The old has passed away; behold, the new has come (2 Cor 5:17). Therefore by Christ we are admitted into the holy precincts of God. "Who may ascend into the hill of the Lord? And who may stand in His holy place? He who has clean hands and a pure heart" (Ps 24:3–4).

> Therefore, since we have a great high priest who has passed through the heavens, Jesus the Son of God, let us hold fast our confession. For we do not have a high priest who cannot sympathize with our weaknesses, but One who has been tempted in all things as we are, yet without sin. Therefore let us draw near with confidence to the throne of grace, so that we may receive mercy and find grace to help in time of need. (Heb 4:14–16 NASB)

In Genesis chapter 4 we are notified that "Cain worked the soil." In Genesis chapter 1 we are informed that God said, "Let the land produce living creatures," which began the process from which humankind eventually evolved. We are reminded of our lowly beginnings in Genesis chapter 2 when Adam is said to be "formed from the dust of the ground." Cain worked the same soil that we were originally taken from. He offered the work of his hands to the Lord but God was displeased. Cain's brother Abel offered "the firstborn of his flock" and was looked on with favor by Yahweh.

Christ's crucifixion exhibited the joint offerings of Cain and Abel: we as humanity have shaped ourselves into an unholy mess. Christ became a part of humanity when he took on our flesh, he presented humanity to the Lord God and the Lord God showed us exactly what he thought of what our hands have shaped. We came from the soil and we have worked that soil and crafted ourselves into an offering that is unacceptable to God. What God made is good, what we ourselves have made is shoddy, substandard, and in a word, evil.

God and Primordial People

A beautiful picture of the kingdom of heaven is captured in Isaiah.

> a highway will be there;
> it will be called the Way of Holiness;
> it will be for those who walk on that Way.
> The unclean will not journey on it;
> wicked fools will not go about on it. (Isa 35:8)

We are the unclean wicked fools, and we cannot walk on that lofty highway, we know of no way of climbing up to it, it is far beyond our reach.

But we remember that the firstborn offering of Abel was well received by Yahweh, and as Christ offered himself as a representative of evil humankind right at the center of that offering was a humble, meek, obedient, and lowly heart. Christ had previously exhorted us to "Take my yoke upon you and learn from me, for I am gentle and humble in heart" (Matt 11:29). The humility at the center of the sacrifice found favor with God and lifts humanity up to the heights of heaven's elevated highways.

Our waywardness can be turned, our uncleanness can be washed, and humanity can be saved. We allowed the serpent to inject his poison into us resulting in humanity's spot and blemish—damaging our spirit and touching our bodies. Something deep within us is wrong; body, soul, and spirit are affected. But Christ has enabled humanity to once again put ourselves in God's hands. We began to turn away from God many years ago and one of the first moves we made was to replace the relationship we had with God and exchange it for manmade idols. But through Christ we can renew that relationship with God. "Then I will sprinkle clean water on you, and you will be clean; I will cleanse you from all your filthiness and from all your idols" (Ezek 36:25). And even our bodies, through Christ's resurrected life, can lose their "spot." "Let us draw near with a sincere heart in full assurance of faith, having our hearts sprinkled clean from an evil conscience and our bodies washed with pure water" (Heb 10:22).

> Praise the Lord, my soul; all my inmost being, praise his holy name. Praise the Lord, my soul, and forget not all his benefits—who forgives all your sins and heals all your diseases. (Ps 103:1–3)

Chapter 26

A Clean Heart

KING DAVID CAME FACE to face with his own blemish when the prophet Nathan approached him and told him the scenario of a rich man who had many sheep and a poor man who had one lamb. The rich man took the poor man's lamb. The story compelled David to cry out, "He must pay for that lamb four times over, because he did such a thing and had no pity." Nathan then spoke the shuddering words, "You are the man!" (2 Sam 12). David had taken the wife of Uriah the Hittite and had disposed of Uriah using the army as a cover—Nathan exposed David's sinful folly.

David was left to contemplate his own spot and blemish. "Surely I was sinful at birth, sinful from the time my mother conceived me" (Ps 51:5). He reaches out to God and cries, "Create in me a clean heart, O God; and renew a right spirit within me" (Ps 51:10 KJV). David's renewal of spirit extended back to when God first created humankind in his image—upright, trustworthy, and faithful. Uriah may not have been an Israelite, a factor that may have been in David's reasoning when he first lay down with Bathsheba, Uriah's wife. But God's sceptre reaches to all men regardless of race or creed: injustice will demand recompense in his eyes.

David also knew that creating a clean heart in exchange for the corrupt heart we each inherited from our forefathers was within God's reach. In Psalm 103 David begins by speaking to his own diseased soul. Praise the Lord, my soul, and forget not all his benefits—who forgives all your sins and heals all your diseases, who redeems your life from the pit and crowns you with love and compassion, who satisfies your desires with good things so that your youth is renewed like the eagle's (2–5).

Humanity's youth can be renewed. In those far off days of primeval humanity, when the first human beings received their spirit from the breath of God, their commission was simple: multiply in number, have dominion over the animals, and eat food provided by God. Exactly how the human beings went about these God-given directives was left up to them to decide. There were no laws written down and no guidelines. If we understand that modern humans have been on this earth for 200,000 years, then we realize that it is only very recently that we have received biblical commandments. God, by and large, leaves the inner-workings of society to us. We have the "know-how" because we are made in his image. So the practical nature of putting righteousness into practice is left up to us, God expects us to understand what the righteous course of action is as a part of the package of being made in his likeness. Written laws and bylaws can sometimes become a quagmire, causing English dramatist George Chapman in 1654 to give us the phrase "the law is an ass," a phrase used by many bright and intelligent people ever since. The "spirit of the law" is what counts. If a man gets his lady pregnant, righteousness demands that the man provides and protects for his woman while she is giving birth and weaning the child. The child will also appreciate the presence of a loving man as a father. These are laws written into the hearts of men and women, we don't need them written down for us—we know them. The male who produces progeny and runs away is thought of as a worthless individual who should be avoided by all decent females. There are numerous laws that we know without having to see them written down. Jesus stated this succinctly when he said, "Do to others as you would have them do to you" (Luke 6:31). We may call this common sense, or what the philosophers call "the Natural Law," natural because we all have it by nature, or we may call it the "spirit of the law."

Some people may not care about doing "the right thing" and some may not believe in right or wrong at all. However, many people at some point in their lives will call out for justice, maybe their mobile phone has been stolen or someone has injured them whilst driving with too much alcohol in their blood or perhaps someone has defamed them or said things about them that are not for other peoples' ears. The Natural Law is on the hearts of humans but the fall of humanity can eventually bury the Natural Law deeply and not allow it to surface.

King David wrote Psalm 40:8 where he states, "your law is within my heart," which of course is the exact place the law should be. Sin's presence in our human makeup gave rise to God physically writing laws on tablets of stone—symbolic of the laws he first wrote on our hearts but now our hearts are hard like stone. We could see, hear, and understand the laws written on stone, which were written in the hope that we would once again change our direction and turn towards our creator. God wrote the law so that "people are without excuse." God will enliven our conscience as we change our way of thinking and repent. Through Christ, humanity's hope returns so that, as God told Jeremiah, "I will put my law in their minds and write it on their hearts" (Jer 31:33). Then the "spirit of the law" will once again take its rightful place in our hearts.

Since we became spoiled by sin we did not always apply the "spirit of the law." We lived selfishly and made ourselves ill fit for the universe we inhabit. Christ's act of demolishing what we ourselves have created by his death on the cross enables us to "put on the new self, which is being renewed in knowledge in the image of its Creator" (Col 3:10). Leaving Solomon to proclaim,

> Thou art all fair, my love; there is no spot in thee. (Song 4:7 KJV)

Or as the New American Standard Bible puts it,

> You are altogether beautiful, my darling, And there is no blemish in you.

Christ's death and resurrection has achieved that for the human race. "Praise be to the God and Father of our Lord Jesus Christ! In his great mercy he has given us new birth into a living hope through the resurrection of Jesus Christ from the dead, and into an inheritance that can never perish, spoil or fade. This inheritance is kept in heaven for you" (1 Pet 1:3–4).

> Love divine, all loves excelling,
> joy of heaven, to earth come down;
> fix in us thy humble dwelling;
> all thy faithful mercies crown!
> Jesus thou art all compassion,
> pure, unbounded love thou art;
> visit us with thy salvation;
> enter every trembling heart.
>
> Finish, then, thy new creation;
> pure and spotless let us be.
> Let us see thy great salvation
> perfectly restored in thee;
> changed from glory into glory,

till in heaven we take our place,
till we cast our crowns before thee,
lost in wonder, love, and praise.

CHARLES WESLEY, 1707–1788

"Christ loved the church and gave himself up for her to make her holy, cleansing her by the washing with water through the word, and to present her to himself as a radiant church, without stain or wrinkle or any other blemish, but holy and blameless" (Eph 5:25–27).

Appendix A

WORKING BACKWARDS, ACCORDING TO the Septuagint the patriarchal timeline looks like this:

Solomon begins building the temple in 966 BC. (Then add the 440 years of 1 Kings 6:1.)

The exodus occurs in 1406 BC. (The law was issued 50 days after the exodus.)

Galatians 3:16–18 informs us that the promise to Abraham came 430 years before the law.

Abraham received his first promise in the city of Ur (Gen 12:1). Stephen confirms this in Acts 7:2.

The sojourning of the children of Israel, who dwelt in Egypt and Canaan (LXX) lasted 430 years (Exod 12:40).

"At the end of the 430 years, to the very day, all the Lord's divisions left Egypt" (Exod 12:41).

The words "to the very day" indicate that Abraham's journey began on 14th Abib 1836 BC.

(This is also confirmed by the Lord who said to Abraham, "Know for certain that for 400 years your descendants will be strangers . . . " [Gen 15:13]. Starting from the birth of Isaac, who was Sarah and Abraham's offspring, there would be 400 years until Abraham's descendants were free, which happened at the exodus. Abraham left Haran when he was 75 years old [Gen 12:4], leaving us to conclude that he was 70 when he left the city of Ur. Abraham was 100 when Isaac was born, giving us 430 years—30 years from the city of Ur to the birth of Isaac and 400 years from the birth of Isaac to the exodus.)

Appendix A

Therefore Abraham was born in 1906 BC. (He was 70 years old when his journey began.)

Terah was born in 2036 BC. (Terah was 130 when Abraham was born.)

Nahor was born in 2115 BC. (Nahor was 79 when he fathered his first son. This figure is taken from the Septuagint "Codex Alexandrinus," which has the full genealogies in Genesis 5 and 11. "Codex Vaticanus," which is the version of the Septuagint held in the Vatican, has 179 years for Nahor's age at the birth of his first son.)

Serug was born in 2245 BC. (Age 130 at birth of son.)
Reu was born in 2377 BC. (Age 132 at birth of son.)
Peleg was born in 2507 BC. (Age 130 at birth of son.)
Eber was born in 2641 BC. (Age 134 at birth of son.)
Shelah was born in 2771 BC. (Age 130 at birth of son.)

Arphaxad was born in 2906 BC. (We need to notice that Genesis 11:10 says, "Two years after the flood, when Shem was 100 years old, he became the father of Arphaxad." Arphaxad was 135 at the birth of his son.)

The flood occurred in 2908 BC. (Coinciding with the archaeological and geological flood deposits.)

Shem was born in 3006 BC. (Shem was not Noah's firstborn—"Noah was 500 years old, he became the father of Shem, Ham and Japheth" [Gen 5:32]. [Shem is mentioned first because he is important to the continuing story.] Arphaxad was born two years after the flood when Shem was 100 so Noah was 502 when Shem was born. Noah was 600 when the flood came [Gen 7:6]. Japheth's birth preceded Shem's birth by two years. Japheth is called "the elder" in Genesis 10:21 and Ham is called the "youngest" in Genesis 9:24.)

Noah was born in 3508 BC. (Age 500 at birth of son.)
Lamech was born in 3696 BC. (Age 188 at birth of son.)
Methuselah was born in 3863 BC. (Age 167 at birth of son.)
Enoch was born in 4028 BC. (Age 165 at birth of son.)
Jared was born in 4190 BC. (Age 162 at birth of son.)
Mahalaleel was born in 4355 BC. (Age 165 at birth of son.)
Cainan was born in 4525 BC. (Age 170 at birth of son.)
Enosh was born in 4715 BC. (Age 190 at birth of son.)
Seth was born in 4920 BC. (Age 205 at birth of son.)
Adam was born in 5150 BC. (Age 230 at birth of son.)

Bibliography

Center for the Advanced Study of Human Paleobiology. "CASHP Researchers Show Neandertals Had Varied Diet, Cooked Plant Foods." December 28, 2010. https://cashp.columbian.gwu.edu/cashp-researchers-show-neandertals-had-varied-diet-cooked-plant-foods.

Gibbons, Ann. "The Evolution of Diet." *National Geographic* 226:3 (September 2014) 34–53. http://www.nationalgeographic.com/foodfeatures/evolution-of-diet/.

Goucher, Candice, and Linda Walton. *World History: Journeys from Past to Present.* 2nd ed. New York: Routledge, 2013.

Harari, Yuval Noah. *Sapiens: A Brief History of Humankind.* London: Harvill Secker, 2014.

Hesiod. *Homeric Hymns, Epic Cycle, Homerica.* Translated by Hugh G. Evelyn-White. Loeb Classical Library, vol. 57. London: William Heinemann, 1914.

Kaufman, Scott Barry. "Gorillas Agree: Human Frontal Cortex is Nothing Special." *Scientific American* (May 16, 1013). https://blogs.scientificamerican.com/beautiful-minds/gorillas-agree-human-frontal-cortex-is-nothing-special/.

Kirkbride, Diana. "Umm Dabaghiyah." In *Fifty Years of Mesopotamian Discovery: The Work of the British School of Archaeology in Iraq, 1932–82,* edited by John Curtis, chap. 1. Hertford, England: Stephen Austin, 1982.

Koerth-Baker, Maggie. "Who Lives Longest?" *New York Times Magazine* (March 19, 2013). http://www.nytimes.com/2013/03/24/magazine/who-lives-longest.html.

Little Richard. "He Got What He Wanted." Written by Richard W. Penniman, arranged by Roger Blackwell. Chicago: Mercury, 1962.

Macrae, Fiona. "We're All Getting Smaller and Our Brains Are Shrinking . . . Is Farming to Blame?" *DailyMail.com* (June 12, 20ll). http://www.dailymail.co.uk/sciencetech/article-2002684/Were-getting-smaller-brains-shrinking-farming-blame.html.

McIntosh, Jane R. *Ancient Mesopotamia: New Perspectives.* Understanding Ancient Civilizations. Santa Barbara, California: ABC-CLIO, 2005.

NIH/National Human Genome Research Institute. "Researchers Trim Count of Human Genes to 20,000–25,000." *ScienceDaily* (October 21, 2004). www.sciencedaily.com/releases/2004/10/041021075155.htm.

Norman, Larry. "Déjà vu—If God Is My Father." Written by Larry Norman. Salem, Oregon: Solid Rock Records, 1976.

Norton, F. C. *A Popular Handbook of Assyriology,* s.v. "Garden of Eden." Ditchling, Sussex: F. C. Norton, 1908.

Bibliography

Owen, James. "Bone Flute is Oldest Instrument, Study Says." *National Geographic News* (June 24, 2009). http://news.nationalgeographic.com/news/2009/06/090624-bone-flute-oldest-instrument.

Potts, Daniel T. *Mesopotamian Civilization: The Material Foundations*. Great Britain: Cornell University Press, 1997.

Poulton, Paul. "Let Your Foot Fall." Poem written by Paul Poulton. United Kingdom: copyright, 2017.

Pringle, Heather. "The First Americans." *Scientific American* (2017). https://www.scientificamerican.com/article/the-first-americans/.

Ryan, Timothy M., and Colin N. Shaw. "Gracility of the Modern *Homo Sapiens* Skeleton is the Result of Decreased Biomechanical Loading." Edited by Clark Spencer Larsen. Proceedings of the National Academy of Sciences of the United States of America (PNAS) (November 20, 2014). http://www.pnas.org/content/112/2/372.abstract.

Streily, Andrea Hansen. "Early Pottery Kilns in the Middle East." *Paléorient* 26 (2000) 69–81. http://www.persee.fr/doc/paleo_0153-9345_2000_num_26_2_4711.

Streit, Katharina. "Re-evaluating the Ubaid: Synchronizing the 6th and 5th Millennia BC of Mesopotamia and the Levant." MA thesis, Institute of Archaeology, Hebrew University of Jerusalem, 2012. http://www.academia.edu/3751066/Re-evaluating_the_Ubaid_Synchronizing_the_6th_and_5th_millennia_BC_of_Mesopotamia_and_the_Levant_unpublished_MA_thesis_.

Vecchierello, Hubert. *Einstein and Relativity: Lemaître and the Expanding Universe*. Paterson, New Jersey: St. Anthony Guild Press, 1934.

Wheeler, John. "Information, Physics, Quantum: The Search for Links." In *Complexity, Entropy, and the Physics of Information*, edited by Wojciech Hubert Zurek, chap. 19. Redwood City, California: Addison-Wesley, 1990. https://jawarchive.files.wordpress.com/2012/03/informationquantumphysics.pdf.

Wood, Frank, et al. "Salt (NaCl)." In *Encyclopaedia Britannica*. Posted July 26, 1999. https://www.britannica.com/science/salt.

Zarins, Juris. Review of *The Early History of the Ancient Near East: 9000–2000 BC*, by Hans J. Nissen. Translated by Elizabeth Lutzeier, with Kenneth J. Northcott. *Journal of the American Oriental Society* 112:1 (January–March 1992) 55–57. http://www.jstor.org/stable/604585?seq=3#page_scan_tab_contents.

Zohary, Daniel, et al. *Domestication of Plants in the Old World: The Origin and Spread of Cultivated Plants in West Asia, Europe, and the Nile Valley*. 4th ed. Oxford, UK: Oxford University Press, 2012.

www.ingramcontent.com/pod-product-compliance
Lightning Source LLC
Chambersburg PA
CBHW050825160426
43192CB00010B/1900